BARTS AND THE LONDON
SCHOOL OF MEDICINE AND DENTISTRY
WHITECHAPEL LIBRARY,TURNER STREET, LONDON E1 2AD
020 7882 7110

4 WEEK LOAN
Book are to be returned on or before the last date below,
otherwise fines may be charged.

LEADING IN THE NHS

Also by Rosemary Stewart

THE REALITY OF MANAGEMENT
*THE REALITY OF ORGANIZATIONS
*MANAGERS AND THEIR JOBS
*HOW COMPUTERS AFFECT MANAGEMENT
CONTRASTS IN MANAGEMENT
CHOICES FOR THE MANAGER
THE BOSS: The Life and Times of the British Businessman
   (*with Roy Lewis*)
THE DISTRICT ADMINISTRATOR IN THE NATIONAL HEALTH SERVICE
   (*with Peter Smith, Jenny Blake and Pauline Wingate*)

*Also published by Macmillan

Leading in the NHS

A Practical Guide

Rosemary Stewart

MACMILLAN

First published 1989

Published by
THE MACMILLAN PRESS LTD
Houndmills, Basingstoke, Hampshire RG21 2XS
and London
Companies and representatives
throughout the world

Printed and bound in Great Britain at
The Camelot Press Ltd, Southampton

British Library Cataloguing in Publication Data
Leading in the NHS: a practical guide
1. Great Britain. Health services.
Management
I. Title
362.1′068
ISBN 0–333–48084–8 (hardcover)
ISBN 0–333–48085–6 (paperback)

Contents

List of Figures

Acknowledgements

This book stems from what I have learnt in my discussions and interviews over the years with people in the NHS in a variety of studies including the most recent, the Templeton tracer study of District General Managers (DGMs); I am grateful to them for their interest and help. (The National Health Service Training Authority (NHSTA) funded this tracer study of twenty district managers from the spring of 1985 to the autumn of 1987, and it was published by them as the Templeton Series on District General Managers.) This book draws upon that study. The views expressed are my own and not necessarily those of the NHSTA.

I am especially grateful to my two research associates on the Templeton project, Sue Dopson and Dr John Gabbay, for their great contribution in all respects to that research and to the nine Issue Studies that came from it (see Appendix A). However, the views expressed in this book may not necessarily be theirs. I am most grateful, too, for their many contributions to the research, to Professor Derek Williams who was consultant to the project and to Peter Smith who was a part-time research associate to the project and with whom I have had the pleasure of working on earlier studies in the NHS.

The DGMs who attend the Templeton DGMs' workshop, which has been meeting since the early days of general management, have helped to keep me up to date with the concerns of DGMs and have provided an opportunity to discuss some of the issues that arose during the tracer study.

It was a pleasure to interview the young leaders described in Chapter 9, and I am encouraged by what I heard. There is clearly some good young talent getting into middle and senior management posts. I owe a particular debt to the DGM who is the subject of Case Study 4, and who provides such a good example of leadership in action.

I am grateful also to the following who have read and commented helpfully upon part or all of the book at the draft stage: Pat Duff, Sue Dopson, who alone has borne the burden of reading and criticising more than one draft of the book, Dr John Gabbay, Christine Hancock, Dr Deborah Hennessy, Charles Kaye, Dr Bill McQuillan, Mike Marchment, Leslie Paine, John Smyth and Professor Derek

Williams. Of course the responsibility for the views expressed, and for the remaining defects, are mine. I am grateful to Valerie Martin for her willing and efficient help at all stages. I am also grateful to my Amstrad, and to Word, for making writing a book so much easier, despite the technical hitches.

ROSEMARY STEWART

Guide to Reading This Book

Readers from different backgrounds, and at different stages in their career, can use this book, but they should use it differently, hence this guide.

1. *If you want to skim the book* – Read the Introduction, Contents page, Summary and **bold type** passages of Chapter 1, the Summaries of the chapters that interest you, and the comments 'In Conclusion' (p. 185).
2. *If you only want to read what is most relevant to you* – Everyone read the Introduction, Contents page, comments 'In Conclusion' (p. 185) and at least the Summary of Chapter 1.

Who you are	What to read
Junior and middle managers in any profession including administration	Chapters 1, 2, 9, 10, 11, 12 **Bold type** passages and Summaries of Chapters 3, 4, 8
Senior nurses	Chapters 1, 2, 3, 11, 12 **Bold type** passages and Summaries of Chapters 4, 8 If you like Case Studies, read Chapters 9 and 10 – Case Study 1 is of a hospital manager who is a nurse
Doctors	Chapters 1, 4 and **bold type** passages and Summary of Chapter 3 Chapters 11 and 12 for those involved in management
General managers and other senior managers	Chapter 1 Start with the Summary of each chapter, and then read the chapters that interest you

Chairman, Vice-Chairman	Chapters 1, 3, 4, 5, 6 Summary of Chapters 7, 8 You may find the Case Study in Chapter 10 interesting to compare with your DGM
Members	Chapters 3, 4, 6, 8, 10
Those involved in management development in the NHS	Chapters 1, 9–12 and the chapters on relationships that are relevant to those with whom you are working
Students	Chapters 1, 2, 9, 10, 11, 12 and any of the others relevant to your course
Others working with the NHS	Chapter 8 You may also find Chapter 10 of interest
Others	Chapters 1, 2, 11, 12 are of value to managers in other organisations and to management students

Glossary of Acronyms

CHC   Community Health Council
CNO   Chief Nursing Officer
DA   District Administrator
DGM   District General Manager
DHA   District Health Authority
DMO   District Medical Officer
DMT   District Management Team
DNA   District Nursing Adviser
DNO   District Nursing Officer
FPC   Family Practitioner Committee
GP   General Practitioner
IHSM   Institute of Health Services Management
IPR   Individual Performance Review
JCC   Joint Consultative Committee
MEC   Medical Executive Committee
MP   Member of Parliament
MSC   Manpower Services Commission
NAHA   National Association of Health Authorities
NHS   National Health Service
NHSTA   National Health Service Training Authority
OPCS   Office of Population Censuses and Surveys
OT   Occupational Therapist
RGM   Regional General Manager
RHA   Regional Health Authority
RMO   Regional Medical Officer
UGM   Unit General Manager

Introduction

This book has a mission. This mission is to persuade you, the reader, that the NHS needs leadership and that you should be leading, and preparing yourself to be a better leader. There *are* opportunities for leadership even in junior jobs. My mission is also to help you to understand leadership, to think boldly about what you could achieve and to suggest ways of doing so. It is a guide to leading the different groups that make up the NHS.

My aim is to encourage you to think highly of your role, to lift your head above the immediate pressures and to see yourself as a *leader*. My message is for present and potential leaders at all levels in the NHS and in all occupations. It is also for Authority members, as you can encourage your managers to be leaders, as well as at times making a leadership contribution yourself.

This book is written because I believe – passionately – that leadership at all levels in the NHS is required to overcome the defeatist tendencies that have been a characteristic of the NHS over the years.[1]

In 1984–5 the introduction of general management into the NHS led to a major reorganisation. The 1989 NHS review means more radical change. Leadership is now both more necessary, and more possible, than in the past. Management and administration remain necessary and it is important that they are well done. What is new is the growing need for leadership to help staff, whatever their professional background, to tackle the new situations with which they are faced.

Most books for NHS readers are about functions like planning, about resource allocation or structures. Surprisingly few are about the *people* in the NHS.[2] Yet the work of organisations gets done mainly through people, particularly in a service like the NHS. Changes affect people and to be implemented successfully require their support. Enthusiastic commitment and well directed energy are the marks of well led organisations that cope successfully with changes whatever their cause. Leadership can generate this commitment: leaders to do this are needed at all levels in the NHS.

The book originates from a two and a half year study, from 1985–7, of a sample of 20 District General Managers (DGMs) in the NHS in England and Wales,[3] from an earlier study of District Administrators

(DAs),[4] from a current study of changes affecting middle managers in all kinds of organisations, and from the author's experience of teaching managers in industry, commerce and the public service (including the NHS), how to review their effectiveness. The author has also co-directed an international conference on leadership.[5]

Part I, Chapter 1 describes the *concept* of leadership, and how it differs from management and administration, though all three are needed in the NHS. Part II is about *how to lead* the different kinds of individuals and groups with whom leaders in the NHS may have to work. Its introduction describes five common reasons for friction, and gives some general guidance on managing relationships and managing change. Each of the chapters in Part II has a common format:

1. A statement of the *ideal to aim at*.
2. *Difficulties* likely to be encountered in achieving the ideal.
3. Steps to be taken towards achieving the ideal.

These steps are based on the experience of leaders in the NHS and in other organisations. You can use the statement of the ideal as a checklist of points when deciding on *your own*. You can use the account of the difficulties as a warning of those problems you may need to *overcome*. The statement of steps to be taken will help you to decide how to *achieve* your ideal.

Part III gives *practical examples* of leadership in the NHS. Chapter 9 is based on interviews with fifteen young leaders in different occupations within the NHS and at different levels. Twelve of these are discussed together with individual illustrations, and three are longer accounts of how the individual describes and then goes about leading. These are Case Studies 1–3, which have questions at the end so that you can consider their relevance for you. Chapter 10 is a more detailed Case Study of a DGM which describes both his own views on, and his practice of, leadership and how his main contacts described and assessed his approach. The accounts of young leaders are there to encourage young readers to follow their example, and older managers to remember the importance of identifying and developing potential leaders. The Case Studies are there as examples of how different leaders tackle their jobs.

Part IV is intended to help you to become a *more effective leader*. Chapter 11 is about managing yourself and your job, and provides a variety of suggestions and models for doing so. It is therefore about management as well as leadership. It emphasises the need to *improve your understanding* – of yourself, of your job and of ways of becoming more effective in your job. Chapter 12 is about how to develop yourself. The final comments, In Conclusion, are intended to encourage you to *act* on what you have read.

Knowing how busy you are, the book is designed to be read in two ways: to be *skimmed* for its main messages or to be *read* for its detailed help in deciding what you want to achieve, what difficulties you will have to overcome, and how to go about it. The Guide to Reading This Book on pp. ix–x will help you to identify the sections that are most relevant to you, depending on your position.

References are mainly given to acknowledge a quotation, or when the reader may be looking for help. The book is addressed to you, not to fellow academics, though they may find some sections useful for teaching in managerial programmes.

The book follows others in avoiding exclusive use of 'he' for men and women by the use of both 'she' and 'he', by the use of the plural, and sometimes of 'he and she'. I have used the term 'Chairman' because that is still the official description for men and women who are appointed to chair their Authorities.

Templeton College, Oxford   ROSEMARY STEWART
February 1989

Part I

The Concept of Leadership

1 Leadership

'A few years ago I could not have used the word "leadership" without wincing and blushing, now I do use it.' (RGM)

LEADERSHIP, MANAGEMENT AND ADMINISTRATION

In difficult times, people need leadership as well as management. This is true in the NHS today, and in the foreseeable future. It is true, too, in many other organisations in Britain and elsewhere. Yet 'leadership' is a word that many in the NHS are chary of using,[1] even 'management' is often viewed with scepticism and the traditional term, 'administration' preferred. Each word has a different, though often ambiguous, meaning and each is necessary in the NHS today. Before we can focus on leadership, we must first understand how these terms differ.

The definitions below are more clear cut than is customary. In common usage, 'management' and 'administration' are often used interchangeably so are 'management' and 'leadership', and there are no generally agreed definitions. The three terms are sharply distinguished here because there are different roles to be performed that must be clarified if we are to understand the change that is needed in the NHS.

Leadership

The word 'leadership' has an emotive character that 'management' and 'administration' lack, and usually the emotions are positive ones. Most of us think that we can recognise leadership, though we may not find it easy to define.

Leadership is *discovering the route ahead* and encouraging and – personality permitting – inspiring others to follow. Hence leadership is most needed in changing times, when the way ahead is not clear. A good leader should both show the way and make others feel enthusiastic about following it. Change can then, depending on its nature, become positive, exciting and challenging rather than discouraging and threatening.

3

Managers have subordinates. Leaders have followers: people who recognise and find attractive the leader's sense of purpose. Leaders are those who can get the people with whom they work, whether subordinates or not, to be convinced cooperators. Leaders make others feel that what they are doing matters and hence makes them feel good about their work. Taking this description as a guide, look around you at work and ask yourself: 'who are the leaders?' Who are enthusiastic about what they want to do and convey that enthusiasm to others? Leadership should be fun, some of the time, both for the leader and for the followers.

Management

Good management is also important for the NHS. This has increasingly been realised, and was a major reason for the Griffiths reorganisation. Good management makes it possible for the leader's vision to be implemented by providing the discipline of objectives, targets and reviews to make the vision *concrete*. Management is different from leadership, though leadership is an aspect of management; an aspect that is essential in changing situations and less important in stable periods.

Mangement is a set of techniques and approaches that can be learnt. It involves planning, which includes strategy and setting objectives. There are textbooks that tell you how to *plan* and about the related process of *budgeting*. **Organising, in the sense of creating formal structures and procedures, is also part of management.** Textbooks can help the manager to decide what form of organisation is appropriate – for example, what kind of grouping will best suit the tasks to be done and the environment in which they have to be carried out. **Motivating and controlling are two other classic management functions, along with coordination.** Management textbooks and management consultants can advise on *motivational strategies*, on the techniques for *controlling* and on the methods of *coordination*. Plenty of such textbooks exist, including two by the author,[2] so this book does not describe such managerial functions.

The NHS has been deficient in the knowledge and practice of management, though these are essential for the effective use of resources. Gradually its officers – significantly now more often called 'managers' – have been learning to think more like managers: to recognise the importance of deciding what has to be done and of ensuring that it gets done by agreeing objectives, establishing priorities and target dates, and monitoring whether plans are being implemented. Gradually, too, managers in the NHS are learning to be more concerned with cost effectiveness. More slowly, they are recognising the influence that they have on *staff motivation* and their responsibility for *creating an environment* where staff feel well motivated. This is where leadership rather than purely managerial ability can help.

Administration

In the past, only administration was thought to be necessary in public service; hence the public service had administrators and companies had managers and sometimes leaders too. **Administration is the carrying out of policies, and being publicly accountable for doing so.** Public accountability means that administration involves more paperwork than management because there needs to be *written evidence* of what is done, and why.

Administration in the NHS has also had the task of providing a service to the carers, who require and deserve efficient administration. This requirement has not changed nor has the public accountability. So administration is still needed. Managers should ensure that there is efficient administration. It will often be done more efficiently by one of their staff, provided they choose the right person, than by themselves. **Good managers are not necessarily good administrators, and a leader has a more important role to play away from the desk.**

1. Administrators **confirm in writing**.
2. Managers **direct**.
3. Leaders **point the way**: they identify and symbolise what is important.

These descriptions personify the different approaches involved, though leaders will also have to manage. There are situations – though rare in the NHS today – where leadership is not required. Whether you need to lead as well as to manage depends upon which of the following is your most important responsibility:

1. stability, so managing *variations*;
2. managing *improvement*;
3. *radical change*.

Administrators should be able to cope with the first, maintaining stability, managers with the second. It is *leaders* who are needed for more radical change and for coping with a difficult environment.

CHARACTERISTICS OF LEADERSHIP

Pointing the Way

This is the leader's *first task*. The DGM in Case Study 4 uses the analogy of an arrow to describe his leadership role. Leaders can point the way only if they *know the direction that they want to go*. When you start in a new job, it may be all too clear to you what needs to be changed. Sometimes that will not be so; if you have been in the job a long time you may not see any new paths ahead. Subsequent chapters suggest the ideals to aim at which you can use as a starting point.

It helps to have a picture – what in writings on leadership is called a 'vision' – of where we want our part of the organisation to be in the future. (It is not only writers who use that word – Shell, for example, has been using 'visioning' as a process for some years.) Warren Bennis and Burt Nanus in their book on leadership explain what a vision is as follows:

> 'a vision articulates a view of a realistic, credible, attractive future for the organization, a condition that is better in some important ways than what now exists . . . With a vision, the leader provides the all-important bridge from the present to the future of the organization.'[3]

They see having a vision of what you want to achieve as distinguishing a leader from a manager:

> 'By focusing attention on a vision, the leader operates on the *emotional and spiritual resources* of the organization, on its values, commitment, and aspirations. The manager, by contrast, operates on the *physical resources* of the organization . . . An excellent manager can see to it that work is done productively and efficiently, on schedule, and with a high level of quality. It remains for the effective leader, however, to help people in the organization know pride and satisfaction in their work.'[4]

Symbolising What Matters

An essential role for a leader is to symbolise the *meaning* and *values* of an organisation – one DGM described himself as the 'keeper of the flame'. It is for this reason that a visible leader is important in encouraging others to contribute wholeheartedly to the goals of the organisation. **A leader shows clearly what he or she cares about.** Peter, the DGM in Case Study 4, led his staff in part by his passionate commitment to the NHS and its task of serving the community.

Getting Others to Share Your Ideals

Leadership means getting people to share the ideals, to attach the same meanings to what is happening and what needs to be done. As Gareth Morgan, a Canadian professor of administrative studies, puts it:

'the process of becoming a leader ultimately hinges on the ability to create a shared sense of reality'.[5]

And also, as Warren Bennis, an American professor, who has written about leadership over many years, says:

'The leader must be a social architect who studies and shapes what is called "the culture of work" – those intangibles that are so hard to discern but so terribly important in governing the way people act, the values and norms that are subtly transmitted to individuals and groups and that tend to create binding and bonding.'[6]

Creating Pride in the Organisation

Leadership involves getting people to identify with their part of the organisation and to feel proud of where they work. This is an aspect of leadership that the armed services understand well, though that understanding may not translate into the very different environment of the NHS.

Pride is linked to achievement and high standards. It is about being able to say – and being enthusiastic about saying – how we excel. Leadership sets high goals and is not content with statements like: 'we compare favourably with', and still less: 'we are no worse than'.

Making People Feel Important

This is closely linked to the next characteristic of leadership, of *realising people's potential*. **People have more energy and will set themselves higher standards if they think that they, and what they do, matter.** Feeling good about what you are doing is a major incentive. Peter in Case Study 4 pp. 143–58 is a good example of a leader who makes people feel like that. It does not require special skill, but an ability to treat each person as a *distinct* and *valued* individual.

Realising People's Potential

Leaders in an organisation should be providing the environment – the *culture* – within which people's energies are released, and they feel able to innovate. This is now described as 'enabling' others to perform, a fashionable word that has its roots in Douglas McGregor's *Theory Y*. Writing in 1960 he said:

> 'the limits on human collaboration in the organizational setting are not limits of human nature but of management's ingenuity in discovering how to realize the potential represented by its human resources'.[7]

This is a lesson that many managers still find it hard to learn despite all the writings, teaching and practical examples that have reinforced it since McGregor wrote.

Leaders do not necessarily have to lead from the front. They can share leadership, as the second part of Chapter 5 on Sharing the Leadership describes. **One of a leader's responsibilities is to develop leadership qualities in others by giving them opportunities to lead.** This means giving them the *space* and the *opportunities* to grow.

Self-sufficiency

Being a leader can be *lonely*. You have to take tough decisions, which may be painful to individuals, and some that are more generally unpopular. So, you must not be too dependent upon being liked. The young leaders in Chapter 9 talked about this, as did many of the DGMs in the tracer study. You will also have to take risky decisions. **You must learn to accept yourself and to rely on yourself.** You have, as Heather-Jane says in Chapter 9, to accept that you did your best.

Leadership requires some innate abilities, but less than is popularly

thought. **Many readers could lead provided they knew what they
wanted to achieve and could communicate that to others.** You can
learn to recognise when leadership is required. You can also develop
your understanding of yourself and of others, which will help you to
be a more effective leader.

WHY LEADERSHIP IS NECESSARY

Much more is now expected of managers in most organisations,
including the NHS, than it was in the past. Hence the need for them
to be leaders who can show the way and help others to adapt
successfully to the changing environment within which they work.
Because the management job is more complex and difficult than it
used to be, managers need to give more thought than in the past to
what they and their staff *should be doing*: to map the way ahead.
Even when this is done, it is easy to lose your way amongst the
luxuriant growth of problems.

The NHS needs leaders to help people to cope – and to cope
without discouragement – with the difficulties that confront it (and,
indeed, any method of providing health care). It needs leaders who
will do much more than that, however, who will think positively
about what they can do to improve the Service, not merely negatively
about how they can survive within limited resources.

The changes affecting the NHS have come from a variety of
sources. Some stemmed from the policies of the Conservative
government under Thatcher; others from the general problems of
providing health care in affluent countries. The common pressures
upon health care whatever the system of provision are well known.
They include the larger number of old people, particularly the very
old, the rise in chronic sickness, developments in medical technology
and the 'iceberg' nature of health care, in that there is so much more
care that people can ask for as their knowledge of what can be done
for them increases. It is these problems that led a conference of
health service academics, from France, the USA, Quebec and
Britain, to publish their proceedings in 1984 under the title *The End
of an Illusion*:[8] the illusion being that it was possible to provide
everyone with all the health care that they wanted. It is not the
purpose of this book to discuss the specific implications of the
changes affecting the NHS, which are well documented elsewhere.

The changes that have been affecting the NHS are part of wider changes affecting other organisations, both in this country and abroad. It is the *extent* and *rapidity* of change affecting many kinds of organisations that makes leadership so important today. This is widely recognised. In the UK, for example, there has been a growth of courses on leadership for managers at all levels. These take many different forms including being tested physically and psychologically in unfamiliar and exhausting conditions. One example of the interest in developing leadership ability at the top is that for some years a one-week programme on top management leadership has been regularly sold out at Templeton College, the Oxford Centre for Management Studies. Another example is the number of new books published in the USA in the late 1980s, a few of which are cited in this book, arguing that American companies urgently need to improve their leadership capacity.

The changes affecting the NHS have some parallels in other organisations, though the changes are often greater elsewhere. There have been, and are, major changes affecting managers in industry and commerce that stem from the great increase in competitive pressure, the internationalisation of business, the threat of acquisition, the rapidity of product change especially in the newer industries, and the growth of information technology.

A common aim of many of the changes both within companies and in the public service is to increase sensitivity to *customer needs*. In companies, this is seen as an important way of competing effectively. In the public service, it has been politically inspired, and is a response to the growth of a more knowledgeable and demanding public leading to the end of 'the grateful society' when the recipients of public service were expected to be grateful for any help they received.

There are three main challenges to leaders in the NHS. First, to envision what *should be done* by them and those who work with them to make their part of the Service better. Second, to realise, as the quotation above from Douglas McGregor says, the *potential in human resources*. Third, to *respond* to a more knowledgeable and demanding public.

FINDING THE WAY FORWARD

'Where there is no vision, the people perish'. (Proverbs xxix.18)

The new demands on managers are reflected in the use of different words for talking about what they need to do. One of these is 'vision': a word that many would have thought to be odd, even quite inappropriate, in the 1970s or even the early 1980s. Now its value is as a spur for thinking more boldly about *what you want to do*.

There is a wide difference between those who have a vision of what a better future for their district, unit, department, section or ward would look like, and a set of objectives and targets for getting there, and those who have not lifted their head above their immediate concerns. These are the extremes; more commonly, managers will have objectives for improving and maintaining the work of their group, be it as wide as a district or just a small department, but lack the *vision* that is necessary for leadership. Setting objectives with target dates and reviewing their accomplishment are an essential part of management, but that is not leadership.

All managers can raise their sights, the first step towards developing a vision, if they ask themselves the 'Father Christmas' question: What would I most like Father Christmas to give me for my group? This can help you to think *what would be the ideal*. It helps also to try and picture what the ideal *would look like*, so that you can know when it has been achieved. Doing so is an aid to setting criteria for judging the steps along the way. Once you have made the ideal as concrete as you can, you can begin to work out how you can best move towards it. It is important to believe that success is possible, while recognising the obstacles that may need to be overcome.

In attracting others to your vision, you need to identify the *values* that underpin it. This is best done with your main subordinates, so that all can contribute and thus feel more committed to the values underlying the vision. This process can be done informally, but at the regional, district, and perhaps also the unit level it can be useful to agree a *written statement*. Doing this helps to clarify common agreement on values, provides a reference point for future action and, if necessary, for criticising action taken. An example of such a formal value statement is the one agreed for the West Midlands RHA at a June 1986 interface seminar of regional managers with the region's DGMs:

Set of Basic Values

The following are statements about some basic values which the RHA and DHAs have agreed should be the foundation of their management philosophy:

1. HEALTH CARE NEEDS – The importance of the health needs of

the community is paramount, and this must be constantly re-emphasised as the principle objective towards which all activity is directed.

2.   CORPORATE IDENTITY – It is important to foster leadership and develop a corporate identity within and between Health Authorities in the West Midlands region. There is value in encouraging a sense of belonging to, and sharing in the work of, the region as a whole.

3.   LEADERSHIP – The RHA has a responsibility to provide leadership to DHAs by clearly articulating policies and objectives, and involving them in the process of defining them.

4.   REPRESENTATION – The RHA has a responsibility to define and represent the interests of the National Health Service in the West Midlands, in relation to national government, commerce and industry, the public sector, the media, patients and the public at large.

5.   CONSENT – There is positive value in seeking, wherever possible, to lead by consent rather than coercion.

6.   HONESTY – The RHA will constantly endeavour to be open and honest in all communications.

7.   PARTICIPATION – There is value in encouraging participation by the Health Service professions and clients/patients in Health Service management.

8.   CREATIVITY – Creativity and innovation in management is valuable, and must be encouraged.[9]

Similar statements of basic values have also been developed in some districts.

A statement of values can be used as the starting point for the first step towards achieving your ideal, that is your vision. One such example was submitted in 1986 for the Health Management Award of *The Health Service Journal*. It described what was done to help to improve the quality of life of the residents in a Swandean hospital for elderly long-stay patients in Worthing. Earlier the DGM and his senior staff had drawn up a statement of values. To make progress towards applying a value statement about patient care, the DGM and the CNO had called an informal lunchtime meeting where they 'brainstormed' ideas for entertaining and interesting patients. To take these ideas forward a group of interested people was set up consisting of the hospital's cook, two occupational therapy workers, a clerical officer, nurse, and porter who were joined by the district's voluntary services organiser, a local journalist and a supplies officer. The group became known as the 'energy team'. Their objective was 'to give patients something to look forward to by introducing a full diary of recreational activities by the time of the hospital's open day in September'.

They enlisted support and voluntary help from many sources. This included getting the MSC to fund a recreation team through the Community Programme and substantial donations from the League of Friends. The patients' day was transformed by the project with opportunities for some form of recreational activity every day of the week. The morale of the staff and the image of the hospital in the community were also raised.

This is an example of how the enthusiasm and commitment of junior staff can be enlisted by top management providing the initial stimulus and encouragement. The vision was a better quality of life for elderly long-stay patients by the provision of varied activities. The objective and target date were agreed. Probably the *key decision* was setting up the mixed group of those known to care about the patients' quality of life. In Case Study 1 in Chapter 9 on Young Leaders, there is also a short account of what Heather-Jane Sears did with the same aim. The two examples show different ways of achieving a similar final aim.

This is a relatively simple example from the many good short-listed submissions for the Health Management Award that have been published in *The Health Service Journal*. Each was about a specific innovation, whereas the *Sunday Times*'s 1988 competition was to find the best district.[10] The judges chose North Manchester. Four criteria suggested by John Harvey-Jones helped to distinguish between the finalists:

1. *relationship* between managers and doctors;
2. *attitude to change* in the organisation;
3. approach to *staff*;
4. *clarity* of the district's objectives.

The first three are essential concerns for a good leader in the NHS and the fourth for a good manager anywhere. An impressive feature of the report in the *Sunday Times* is the variety of innovations cited in hospitals, clinics and community care. To give just one example: the use of chiropodists to provide vitamin D to women over 75 to reduce bone softening, which led to a substantial reduction in broken hips. This illustrates the value of greater flexibility in staff roles. Once leaders can enlist staff's interest in finding new and better ways of doing things, there is – as the North Manchester example shows – opportunity for useful innovation in most activities.

SPOTLIGHTING THE WAY

Statements of value are words, and words can be powerful, but words unsupported by actions are meaningless, or worse because they encourage cynicism. **What you *do* matters more than what you say, because that shows what you really treat as important.** Hence it is no good saying that quality matters, and then spending little or none of your time on it. Tom Peters in *Thriving on Chaos* has some powerful things to say about that:

> 'There is in fact no alternative to you acting as standard bearer for a dramatic strategic shift. You may, if you are chief executive, appoint a "representative" – a "quality czar", for example. But beware. He or she can be no more than your point person, and never a true surrogate. There can be no substitute when it comes to the way the members of the organization assess your priorities and the seriousness of your intent. You are either "on" the topic or you are not.'[11]

> 'What matters is that everyone who works for and with you observes you embracing the topic with both arms – and your calendar. What they need to observe is your obvious, visible and dramatic, determination to batter down all barriers to understanding, and then implementation.'[12]

By 'calendar' Peters means the time that you devote to the subject that you are saying is important.

You need to bear witness to the message that you want to put across by what you *say*, and what you *do*. Take opportunities to repeat the message, to use illustrations of what you mean, and (where you can) exemplify them in what you do. The Case Studies in Chapters 9 and 10 provide some examples: Heather-Jane Sears describes how she demonstrates good nursing as a way of raising standards (pp. 124ff). The DGM in Case Study 2 talks about being deliberately enthusiastic and energetic every day, and the DGM in Case Study 4 talks about using his speech at a retirement party as an occasion not only to show appreciation but also to 'spread some messages'.

All those who want to achieve a general change in attitudes and standards should remember that people respond to *symbols*, for example, a chief executive in an organisation with strong status divisions could symbolise that he did not support them by giving up his reserved parking place. John Harvey-Jones, who was noted for his leadership as chairman of ICI, is talking about symbolic actions when he says in his book on leadership:

> 'There is almost always something in a large organization that can be changed which will give very strong messages . . . In this process of change, small actions have a tremendous catalytic and change effect.'[13]

Some of the DGMs in the tracer study also talked about their awareness in the early days in their new job of how quite small actions could symbolise the way things were going to change. One was making a night visit to the district general hospital, which was seen as the 'ivory tower' actually coming to see what staff had to put up with. Another was saying that a request for locks put in three months ago should be done the next day, and that when it was queried, that it was an order, not the start of an argument as to whose fault it was that it had not been done.

PROBLEMS OF BEING A LEADER

We have been talking about leadership as it should be – the ideal – but there are difficulties inherent in being a leader.

Excessive Expectations

People's expectations of what you can achieve may be *unrealistic*. This comes from the wish to believe that leadership will cure the ills that face an organisation or even a society. The desire to attribute unrealistic power to leaders was shown in an American review of the meaning of leadership. It concluded that leadership is a romantic concept:[14] 'romantic' because of the belief that leaders can control the fates of the organisations in their charge. This belief is a double-edged sword for the leader, because it means that not only success, but also failure, are attributed (probably unduly) to the leader. However, the authors concluded that it is better for people in authority to believe that they can influence events, even if in doing so they exaggerate the extent to which they can control what happens, because this belief encourages them to *initiate* and to *persist*.

Undue Importance Attached to Your Remarks

People may pay too much attention to what you say, so that
something you say casually may be noted and acted upon though you
may not have wanted that. Most famously:

'Who will free me from this turbulent priest?'

Henry II, according to history books, which is said to have led to the
murder of St Thomas Becket.

Attitudes to Dependence

A common problem is the ambivalence that many people feel about
dependence upon the leader. If they still have problems with the
relationship with their parents, either now or in retrospect, the
ambivalence will be worse because you may be seen as a substitute
parent. People can both want to be dependent, because they like to
feel that someone else is coping, and yet resent their dependence
upon you. The paradox for the leader is learning to cope with
people's dependency needs, but without making them dependent. As
one DGM put it:

'You should get on to a basis where they acknowledge your
leadership without feeling dominated by it.'

Isolation

As a leader you can easily become isolated, rather cut off from reality
as it is experienced by those who work for you. This can make it
harder to understand how others are feeling. It can also make you
feel lonely. These are common dangers; fortunately less common are
folies de grandeur – that is, an excessive belief in your own importance. Traditionally the court jester was a guard against this, as he had
a licence to make fun of his master, but all leaders can benefit from
having someone who will challenge them.

Lack of Confidence

Leaders need to inspire confidence in others. This means that you
may often need to appear more confident than you feel – a problem
mentioned by several of the young leaders described in Chapter 9. It

is a problem that usually gets less with age and experience in the job. A number of the Templeton tracer DGMs said that after some time in the job they felt more confident than they did at the start of holding this new job.

STEPS TOWARDS THE IDEAL

These are described in the following chapters about leading in particular relationships, so only a few general guidelines are appropriate here:

1. **Do not be afraid to think of yourself as a leader** – the NHS needs leaders.
2. **You do not have to be superhuman to be a good leader, or even to be charismatic, but you must have a strong belief in what needs doing, a picture – even a vision –** of how you think the unit, department, ward, or whatever you are responsible for managing, **should be.**
3. **You need a willingness to convey that vision to others with enthusiasm and a visible personal commitment to its accomplishment.**
4. It helps to have what Tom Peters and Nancy Austin[15] have called **'passion for excellence'.**
5. **You should take a positive rather than a defeatist attitude to setbacks to your aims.**
6. **You should encourage others, but when you feel discouraged keep it to yourself,** though confiding in a friend or counsellor can be helpful.

SUMMARY

1. The NHS needs leaders so do not be afraid to *think of youself as a leader*. Good management and administration are necessary, too, but it is leadership that will enable people to meet the many challenges facing the NHS.
2. Leaders have a *vision* of what they want to achieve. They point the way and make others enthusiastic about following it. They show clearly what they *care about*, and the values that underlie that.

3.   Leaders are *demanding*: they set high goals. They make people feel proud of where they work. Above all, they make people feel important; they enable them to realise their potential.

4.   There are *problems* about being a leader. People may expect too much. They may attach too much importance to what you say, even to chance remarks. You will have to cope with ambivalent attitudes to dependency. You may feel isolated at times. You may have to appear more confident than you feel.

5.   Don't be put off. **You can be a leader if you have a strong belief in what needs doing and can convey that commitment to others. Remember that what you do matters more than what you say, because it shows what you really treat as important.**

Part II

Leading in
Different Relationships

You should lead your staff, but you will often need to lead *other people* if you are to realise your ideal, your vision. The aim of Part II is to help you to do this. Each chapter is about a particular relationship and how you can lead in that relationship, starting with the most common, and usually the easiest, your *subordinates*.

Each of the chapters in this part has the same three divisions:

1. The *ideal* to aim at.
2. The *difficulties* that commonly exist in achieving the ideal, and why they exist.
3. The *steps* that you can take to *move towards* the ideal.

You should use the suggested ideal to *develop your own*. Check to see which aspects of the ideal described you agree with, what you want to add, and what you want to delete.

Why Relationships can be Difficult

There are *five* common reasons for friction between people:

1. **Their jobs require them to pursue different aims. These will make them look at problems from a different perspective.** A major example in the NHS is, as Catherine Jones, the district physio-therapist in Chapter 9 on *Young Leaders* points out, the difference between the clinician's aim of doing the best for the *individual patient* and the manager's need to consider the priorities for *overall patient care* within resource constraints.
2. **Differences in training and experience** develop distinctive values, ways of looking at the world and language – despite my best efforts, some of the words that I use in this book will be unfamiliar to some readers!
3. **Competition for scarce resources.**
4. **Differences in the power of different groups to influence decisions.**
5. **Personality clashes.**

The first and second reasons pose distinctive problems in the NHS because of the variety of separate professional careers. It is the tradition of *distinctive fiefdoms* – medicine, nursing, and physio-therapy, to name but a few – that makes leadership in general management posts such a challenge. There are changes, but the process is slow and painful. It is also challenging – and therefore interesting to good leaders – to learn how to lead those with other career backgrounds than their own. This does mean learning to understand the way *they see the world*. Chapter 4 on Leadership and Doctors discusses this, but it applies equally to understanding those from other backgrounds.

The third and fourth reasons for friction between people are more acute in the NHS than in many other organisations. The fifth can occur in any organisation, but in the NHS it is, as Chapter 4 on Leadership and Doctors describes, most acute between consultants in the same district.

When you are trying to make a relationship more effective, consider *which of these causes* is contributing to the problems. It is common – and all too easy – to attribute to personality problems that have their main cause in differences in role or in background. Remember that a personality clash will stem at least in part from *your own behaviour*.

Managing Your Relationships

As a leader, you will want to manage your relationships so as to achieve your aims. First you will need to develop a good **network of contacts**. John Kotter highlighted the importance for managers of a network of contacts[1] that they can use to support the changes that they are trying to achieve, or to give them the information that they need. He showed how the general managers that he studied in the USA had a wide and diverse network of contacts, and took trouble to maintain them. Most managers have learnt to do so, but those who are still immersed in the professional aspects of their role often do not recognise how important a supportive network of contacts can be. If this is true of you, it is worth considering *whose support you need, and do not currently have*, to get your job done in the way that you want.

Next you should recognise the need to **manage the expectations** of those whom you are leading. You have expectations of what other people should do; they also have expectations of what *you* should do. John Machin, who with his students has done many studies of the expectations that managers have of each other, has shown that often expectations *do not match*.[2] People mistake what others expect of them and do not recognise – or even if they do, may not accept – other people's expectations. Once you know that a mismatch is likely, you will see the importance of trying to manage expectations so that as far as possible they do match. **You need to make clear to others what *you expect of them*, and seek to understand whether they accept these expectations. You can also try to influence what others *expect of you*.**

Managing Change

Leadership means making changes, often radical changes – otherwise there would be no need for leadership! Most changes affect *people*. If the changes are to be successfully implemented, people must be able and willing to implement them. This is often hard, as one DGM said:

'The problem is not knowing what to do, it is knowing how to get it done.'

The first step is to recognise that *change needs to be managed*. Once you have decided what you want to achieve, you need to work out your *strategy*. What should you tackle first? Heather-Jane in Case Study 1 in Chapter 9 describes how she thought about this. Her advice is that you can get away with more when you are new in a job as people then expect change – new brooms sweep clean. Decide what you can do *now*, and what will *take longer*. Often the delay will be because people do not see the *need* to change. Then you have a long process of *changing their attitudes*: that is a key leadership task. Again Heather-Jane illustrates how she has tackled that, so does Alan in Case Study 2 and Peter in Case Study 4 in Chapter 10. You need to 'sell' your ideas persuasively. You need to find and foster allies. When you want to achieve a particular change, think who is likely to be affected by it and whose support is most necessary.

Choose the *right time*. Some times are better than others for getting changes accepted because people are more open to accepting the need for change. Part of the art of managing change is recognising when something has happened that makes people more willing to accept change. For example, an unexpected major budget deficit may make medical representatives more willing to consider changes to help to balance the books. An unfavourable report on the unit's work can also be a stimulus for accepting change.

There are a number of helpful guides to how to manage change, if you want to pursue this further.[3] An important message of all such guides is that change, if it is to be successfully implemented, must be managed – that is you must *develop a strategy* for how you are going to achieve the change, and particularly how you are going to *enlist the necessary support* for it.

2 Leading Subordinates

'The essential thing in organizational leadership is that the leader's style pulls rather than pushes people on. A pull style of influence works by attracting and energizing people to an exciting view of the future. It motivates by identification, rather than through rewards and punishments.' (Bennis and Nanus)[1]

In most jobs leading subordinates is a key aspect of your leadership. You can help to set the standards and values for their work. You can enable them to give of their best. *You can grow future leaders.*

Leading subordinates is the easiest form of leadership because you have more power to *influence what happens*. It is also easier because they are more likely to be *looking for leadership* than are the other people with whom you work. You have your own experience to draw on as a guide to what to do and what not to do, while remembering that your subordinates may differ from you.

THE IDEAL

The ideal is stated in terms of your attitudes and actions:

1. **You will inspire, or at least enthuse, your immediate subordinates so that they share with you a common vision of what your group should be achieving**, whether the group for which you are responsible is as small as a few people or as large as a district.
2. **You will lead your staff towards a common goal that will override the potential disagreements about their relative roles.** This is particularly important if you are responsible for staff with very different roles,[2] as the DGM is with district managers and UGMs.
3. **You will enable your staff to give of their best towards the accomplishment of this shared goal.** A good import from the US is the word 'empower', because it highlights what a good leader can do to give subordinates the inspiration, energy, enthusiasm and the real responsibility for their work.[3]
4. If you have a large staff **those below your immediate subordinates will have seen and heard you, think that you are accessible to**

them and, unless you are in charge of very many people, will also have **talked to you**. They will know what you stand for and feel proud of 'the boss'. They may show this by telling stories about what you do.

5. **You will be aware of, and skilful in, the different facets of leadership**: leadership of *individuals* in one-to-one contacts, *group leadership* where you need to be like the conductor of an orchestra in encouraging those with different contributions to be heard adequately, but unlike the conductor in that you need not always be the one who is conducting a particular piece (project), and *symbolic leadership* as described in Chapter 1.

6. **You will develop future leaders by giving others opportunities to take the lead, and developing their confidence to do so.**

These are what you can contribute as a leader. Your subordinates also need a good *manager*. This book is about leadership rather than management, so only the attitudes and actions that shape your relationship with your subordinates are listed below. Management systems like objective setting and performance review, although useful management tools, are not part of a discussion of leadership.

You will need some other personal qualities as well:

7. **You will have the confidence in yourself that enables you to delegate, and the ability to assess the abilities of your subordinates and to develop them that enables you to do so with good results.**

8. **You really delegate, so that your subordinates know that they have full responsibility**; you delegate *clearly*, so that subordinates know what they are *expected to do*.

9. **You err on the side of being optimistic about what your subordinates can accomplish.**

10. **Your subordinates know that they can come to you for help and support if they have problems**; as John Harvey-Jones says:

'It is essential in a well-run company that in addition to the feeling of plenty of headroom and space to create and carry out one's job, there should be absolute confidence that those above will support one and that one can always look to them as a resource or as a help.'[4]

It is just as essential that subordinates in the NHS should feel like that.

11. **Both you and your subordinates trust each other and feel supported by the other**, for bosses need support, too.

DIFFICULTIES IN ACHIEVING THE IDEAL

There are three potential sources of difficulty: *you, the situation* and *your subordinates*. Naturally most leaders are more conscious of the difficulties from the second and third of these, and are often unaware of the difficulties that stem *from themselves*.

Those That Come From You

1. There may be **personality defects**, but they are often ones that you may be able to overcome by *learning through experience in challenging jobs*:

(a) **A failure of nerve is one of the most serious, and the reason why many managers are not leaders.** Yet even those with leadership abilities may lose their nerve in face of difficulties and not hold to the course that they started on, without having made a judgement that this is the wisest thing to do.

(b) **A desire to be liked**, even to be seen as 'one of the boys' (or girls), is a weakness, because it can make you unwilling to take tough and, unpopular, decisions.

(c) **But do not glory in being unpopular** – leadership should not equate with martyrdom.

(d) **A pessimistic view of human character, so that you are reluctant to trust your subordinates to achieve.** If this trait is too strongly developed, you are unlikely to be a successful leader.

(e) **Inadequate energy, enthusiasm and drive** to inspire, or at least to encourage, your staff.

2. There are difficulties that can come from the **way that you relate to your subordinates**:

(a) **Poor communication**, either in making clear your expectations or in your ability and interest in listening to what your subordinates have to say.

(b) **Failing adequately to see and treat your subordinates as indi-**

viduals, with different strengths and weaknesses and differences in the amount of direction, guidance and support that they need from you.

(c) **Paying too much attention to one group of staff and too little to another.** This does not mean that all should necessarily have the same amount of attention, but none should feel neglected or see you as inaccessible. This danger can exist in any job but is greatest if you are responsible for different types of staff. The Templeton study of DGMs, for example, found that DGMs differed widely in the attention and importance they attached to UGMs compared with their district staff.[5]

3. Finally there are problems that come from a **failure to be on top of your job**.

(a) **Lack of clarity about goals** and the objectives needed to reach them.

(b) **Getting bogged down in operational problems**, so that you are too busy and preoccupied to give your subordinates the broader view that your position should provide.

From the Situation

It is tempting to attach more blame to the situation than is justified, but there are problems that constrain what the leader can do and therefore the leadership that he or she can provide for subordinates.

1. **The pressures on health services everywhere**, and the financial pressures upon the NHS, make management difficult and provide a challenging situation for leadership.
2. **The absence of an external competitive threat** makes the *need for change* harder to establish.
3. **The culture of the NHS**, and the often inherited belief that improvements can be achieved only with more resources, lowers the level of drive and optimism amongst staff.
4. A different aspect of this culture is a **reluctance amongst some staff to accept the idea of a superior–subordinate relationship**, a reluctance that can be found in other professionally based organisations.
5. **The incentives that can be provided for good performance are limited**, and this matters more where the work itself is not very rewarding. However, the Health Service does have a great

advantage over most other organisations in that contributing, in whatever way, to patient care can be seen to be worthwhile.

6. **It may be hard to recruit people of good calibre** in some occupations and the NHS salary levels may not be competitive for jobs that are in demand outside the Health Service.

There are other situational difficulties for managers in the NHS such as political uncertainties and the extent of central intervention, but they are of less relevance to the leadership of subordinates than to some other relationships.

From Subordinates

Complaining about poor subordinates is a temptation for many managers, so that you should always be chary of this explanation for leadership difficulties. However, some leaders are more fortunate than others. If they have been in the same job for some time part, at least, of that good fortune is likely to be of their own making. One problem may be the strong competition for good staff in your locality.

A common difficulty is **inheriting subordinates who are used to a quite different style**, and find it hard to adapt. They may have been tightly controlled and have become unaccustomed to exercising initiative. You may find that some subordinates resent your getting the post, thinking that you are too young or come from an unsuitable background.

STEPS TOWARDS THE IDEAL

Ask yourself whether you are leading. You may be doing so because you are a natural leader, but you may have the capacity to lead yet have so far limited yourself to management, or even just to administration. So the first step is to assess whether you are *leading* your subordinates or just *directing* and *monitoring* them. The following points provide both a way of assessing how far you are leading and guidance as to what you should do.

Pointing the Way

Leaders have followers: people who share a common vision and are

enthusiastically pursuing it, so that will be one test of whether you are leading. Getting a common vision established will usually take time, so there may first be a very uphill 'selling' job to be done. The Case Studies in Chapters 9 and 10 and the account of the fifteen young leaders in Chapter 9 show how some people have sought to get change accepted; the general guidelines in the introduction to Part II may also be helpful.

Visible Leadership

Leaders should be seen because leadership is personal. You should be away from your desk much of the time. Visible leadership is especially important in a bureaucracy like the NHS. It is, as one of Peter's subordinates in Case Study 4 said, 'the willingness to make oneself personally identifiable'.

The NHS must become less bureaucratic, less paper-bound. Some bureaucracy is inevitable in a politically sensitive public Service but **you should, as far as possible, talk rather than write because it is much more personal and direct**. It also enables you to sense reactions, to respond and to be seen to do so. Sometimes you may want to *confirm* the action agreed in writing.

In relationships with subordinates in the NHS you have more choice of whether you talk or write than in some of the other relationships. Hence you can – and should – choose to talk – and even more *listen* – most of the time. One of the DGMs in the Templeton study said in the final interview that:

> 'I should have gone out and about for three months, looking really thoroughly at the organisation. I should have talked to people in a semi-structured way, sharing their and my thoughts on what we should be doing . . . I would recommend managers to do that even in the second generation of DGMs and beyond.'

The DGMs who had done that felt that doing so was worthwhile.

Your greatest power as a leader is the example that you set. The more your subordinates see you as their leader the more attention they will pay to what you do. Remember that people pay more attention to what you *do* than what you *say* – reread the section on the importance of symbols, pp. 14–15. In Chapter 9 on Young Leaders, some of the individuals describe how they consciously seek to act in a way that they want their subordinates to follow, for example:

'I am deliberately and cynically enthusiastic and energetic every day.' (Case Study 2)

More commonly, the young leaders see themselves as setting an example of high standards of work, and of the opportunities open to those who equip themselves for promotion.

You should remember that some at least of your subordinates **may not have had experience of the standards that you expect**. You will need to show them *by your own example* what you mean. If, for example, you take quick action to remedy something that you are told is wrong, you are illustrating what you mean by responding quickly.

If you are heading a professional group you are a *role model* for the profession. (A role model is someone whom others can use as a good example of how to act in that job, or how to act as a member of that profession.) All leaders should be a model for relationships with subordinates so that theirs can learn – particularly if they are young – how to lead their own staff.

A subordinate of one of the Templeton DGMs paid a tribute to his boss as a good example to follow:

'He leads from the top, he is the leader and he has made us leaders as well. He is leading by his own example because he puts so much into it and is so thoroughly committed to the cause.'[6]

The motivation that such visible commitment can give subordinates is described in Case Study 4.

Balancing Two Aspects of Leadership

Studies of leadership have shown that there are two contrasted aspects to the leader's job: *getting the work done* (that is, ensuring performance), and *showing consideration*. The importance of both of these should be known to you from your own experience of working for bosses.

Ideally a leader should be able to **keep both these aspects in balance**, so that the drive for performance does not ignore consideration, and the desire to be considerate does not weaken the drive for performance. If you are temperamentally much stronger on one than the other, it is important to recognise this, and to ensure that you have a deputy or other senior subordinate who can balance you.

Both aspects of leadership are illustrated in the following quotations:

'He has a very personable, easy-going, friendly style but he is quite a taskmaster . . . everybody is under pressure to perform but that gets appreciation and recognition . . . If he gets the bit between his teeth he stays with it.'

'he has not fallen into the trap of managers who have no mercy if deadlines for a whole range of tasks are not always met. He listens to reason, but that is not to say that he is soft and does not press hard to get deadlines met. The difference is between blind insistence and a flexible manager.' (A subordinate of one of the Templeton study DGMs)[7]

One of Peter's subordinates in Case Study 4 in Chapter 10 said that he sometimes had too high expectations of his staff and expressed frustration if they did not live up to them, which could be discouraging:

'There is a world of difference if somebody says to me: "I am disappointed but I realise you are trying very hard" or "I am disappointed why don't you try harder?"'

That is an example where the drive for performance was seen to be *out of balance* with the need for consideration.

Make People Feel Important

This, it may be remembered, was one of the leadership characteristics discussed in Chapter 1. It is more than showing consideration, though that is part of it. There are several illustrations of Peter's awareness of this in Case Study 4. Relate to the *person* first, before discussing the job. This means when you are visiting your staff, knowing them, taking an interest in what they are doing, and in what are their problems, and showing appreciation of good work. It is often good to do something out of the ordinary to mark your recognition of what they are contributing. Simple courtesies are important, too. We can learn from the French custom of greeting a shop assistant before asking for what is wanted, as a recognition of her as a person.

Adapt to Individuals

You need to do this in the way that you relate to different

subordinates. Some need more encouragement than others; some need more guidance; some are easily hurt, and so on.

You also need to adapt in the sense that John Harvey-Jones describes:

'Companies in the past, have tended to expect that their employees should conform to the wishes of the company. This is becoming less and less practicable as a philosophy of operation, and I believe absolutely that in the future it will be the company that conforms to the individual that attracts and motivates the best people. Companies will have to be more flexible in their demands, to accommodate more and more the individuals' different hopes, wishes and ambitions.'[8]

If this is true for companies who have much greater flexibility in rewarding their staff, it should be even more true for the NHS. Within the bureaucratic constraints, you will have some opportunities to take account of individual differences. **Doing so is one way of showing that you see people as individuals.**

Develop Leaders

One of your most important tasks is to develop leaders of the future. You can do much to encourage others to have the confidence to be leaders, as some of the young leaders in Chapter 9 testify. You can do much, too, to develop your staff by giving them challenging tasks that match their abilities, but remaining supportively in the background.

Leaders have followers but they should also help them to grow into leaders: 'followers' in the sense of being attracted to the leader's sense of purpose, but not in being dominated by the leader's personality.

Encourage Challenge

One of the dangers of being a leader, particularly at the top of your particular pyramid, is that you may become complacent, or just blinkered. Hence you should encourage your staff to *challenge you*. John Harvey-Jones describes this challenging role as follows:

'What we are looking for is what I call constructive no-men . . . who will tell us what I or the company should be doing differently.'[9]

It is often hard to get your staff to challenge you, since they may be hesitant to do so, particularly if you have a forceful personality. Taking your immediate subordinates away for a day or two is a method that many general managers have found helps to encourage a more open and searching discussion of major policy issues and of the problems of working together. More junior leaders who are not in a position to do that can still have a short away time for the same purpose – even if 'away' is only in a conference room – but make clear it is not a normal committee or consultative meeting.

Reread the difficulties that may come from your own behaviour that were described earlier in the chapter. Try to get some *honest feedback* about which of these apply to you.

Finally, use your sense of humour and show that work can be fun, at least some of the time.

SUMMARY

1. Leadership of subordinates is the easiest form of leadership, but carries a great responsibility. The key ideal is that **you will inspire your subordinates to share a common vision of what you should be achieving**. You will enable your staff to give of their best. You will grow future leaders.

2. There are three potential sources of difficulty: *you*, *the situation* and the *subordinates themselves*. Beware of blaming the last two and not recognising the difficulties that *you* may cause.

3. The steps that you can take towards the ideal are first to ask yourself whether you are *leading* or only directing and monitoring your staff? Check how far you *are* leading by the extent to which you do the following:

   – seek to get agreement on a *common vision and values*;
   – set a *visible example*: be seen and known;
   – set *high standards of performance* for yourself and others;
   – balance this with *consideration for your staff*;
   – make people *feel important*;
   – adapt to *individuals' needs and wishes*;
   – develop your staff by *stretching them*, but be supportively in the background;
   – encourage your staff to challenge you; seek to get *honest feedback*.

3 Leadership and Nurses

'listening (especially to those at the front) remains the truest signal that "I take you seriously"'. (Tom Peters)[1]

The ideal to be aimed at in the leadership of, and by, nurses must take account of the ways in which nursing differs from other occupations in the NHS or in private health care. It must take account, too, of what should be supported and maintained and what it is desirable to try to change. The word 'leadership' is used in this chapter as it is described in Chapter 1, so is wider than merely professional leadership. It embraces leadership at all levels, whether by nurses or by general managers.

The characteristics of nursing that affect the leadership task, and which often make it more difficult, are:

1. The professional concerns of *maintaining a code of conduct and of establishing and monitoring standards*, characteristics of all professions but of particular importance for a large group of staff working in direct patient care. The monitoring is made more complex by recruiting nurses of varying abilities from a wide cross-section of the community.
2. The *large size and diversity* of the nursing staff.
3. The predominantly *female* membership, but with an increasing number of men amongst the senior nurses in the NHS.
4. A young and predominantly *short-term workforce* in the acute hospital service.
5. The traditional *subordinacy* of the nurse, in many types of nursing, to the doctor.
6. The *continuous provision* of nursing care over the 24 hours.
7. The *stressful nature* of the work.

The leadership task is also influenced by the reaction of many nurses to the Griffiths reorganisation which started in 1984. The Royal College of Nursing's publicity campaign in 1985 against general management showed the disquiet that many nurses felt at what they saw to be a reduction in the status of nurses and in their ability to get their views heard in top level decision-making. This anxiety and resentment continued even though some senior nurses recognised that they had gained by the opportunity to take on new responsibilities.

Many other changes also affect the ideal for nursing leadership. There are the changes in nurse training resulting from Project 2000 and the threat to nurse recruitment posed by the decline in the number of school leavers and the opening up of wider career opportunities for women. The growing shortage of nurses will bring an increasing reliance on support staff. Then there are the changes affecting the NHS that in turn affect nurses' work. These include changes in the organisation of community care, financial constraints, the pressures brought by shorter stays in hospital, the move to more care provided within the community, the increasing number of old people, the changing nature of disease and increasing use of technology.

THE IDEAL

There are some ideals to aim at that should be common to all leaders, whatever their career background, who are in charge of nurses. These are in addition to the ideals discussed in Chapter 2 about leadership and subordinates.

1. **The way nurses approach their work**
    The quality of care, in all its aspects, receives continued and critical attention.

    Nurses are concerned about the *effectiveness* of what they do. This concern shows itself in a critical approach to nursing methods that is supportive of research into nursing practice and of the implementation of research findings about the best practice.

2. **Senior nurses' attitudes to junior nurses**
    Senior nurses understand the motivations and problems of junior nurses, and how these may have changed from when they started in nursing.

    They create a climate in which nurses feel that they can complain about errors and mismanagement without being labelled as 'troublemakers'.

3. **Nurses' ability to be effectively assertive**

Nurses have the ability and the confidence to express their views cogently in meetings, in individual discussions with managers, and to doctors about their concerns over the treatment of individual patients.

4. **Development and promotion of nurses**
   Performance review highlights nurses with abilities for promotion who should then be given opportunities for development.

(a) Nurses are encouraged to develop their *professional*, and for those who are interested *managerial*, knowledge and understanding.

(b) *Wider career opportunities* are available to nurses both within nursing and in general management.

(c) Nurses have the confidence to go for *promotion* both in nursing and in general management.

(d) Senior nurses exemplify *good nursing practices and attitudes*.

5. **Staffing**
   There are the numbers and kinds of nurses that are needed for different services, and these are used effectively. This ideal has three aspects: assessing staffing needs, using staff effectively and recruiting and retaining nurses.

There are two additional ideals that managers with a *non-nursing* background should aim at:

6. **Nurses are much more directly involved in resource management since nursing is such a large proportion of costs.**

7. **Nursing experience is adequately represented in decision-making that affects patient care.**

DIFFICULTIES IN ACHIEVING THE IDEAL

The difficulties stem in part from the attitudes of others towards nurses, and in part from those of *nurses themselves* which contribute to the formation of others' attitudes. The common *constraint of finance* also limits some – but by no means all – of the actions that can be taken towards achieving the ideal.

Difficulties can be divided into those stemming from the changes in nurses' roles since the Griffiths reorganisation and other (potentially, longer-term) difficulties. The latter are discussed first because of their longer-term significance.

Nursing Attitudes

Assertiveness is now recognised as a necessary aspect of leadership but **nurses often lack assertive skills. They have tended to feel aggrieved, but to lack the self-confidence and the skills to press for their grievances to be remedied.** The reasons for this probably include the following:

1. Most nurses are *women*, who have only recently been encouraged to assert themselves.
2. The *traditionally strong nursing hierarchy*, while providing support, emphasised control and discouraged assertiveness in the more junior levels. Many may be glad to be controlled, as it reduces individual responsibility.
3. The absence of a *well-developed knowledge base*.
4. The traditional *subordinacy of nurses to doctors*.

The usual assumption of the nurses' subordinacy to the doctor probably comes from the traditional male–female role split and from the nature of *nursing education*. There is a conflict between the assumption of subordinacy and the expectation that the nurse will be highly responsible and can be relied upon to observe and intervene appropriately. Nurses also work in areas, such as health visiting, midwifery and nursing homes, where what they do does not arise from medical prescription.

Nursing Education

Nursing education in the UK has emphasised *practical skills*. This form of training has not developed powers of logical argument in speech or on paper, nor has it encouraged a respect for the value of research into the best methods of nursing. The emphasis on training in, and adherence to, *procedures* as the way of ensuring that standards are maintained has not encouraged a questioning approach, or much attention to the development of standards.[2] Basic nurse education may follow tradition despite the changes stemming from the recommendations of Project 2000.

Attitudes of Managers to Nurses

Managers have tended – and still tend – to underrate the contribution

of the nursing viewpoint to decision-making. It is noteworthy that in the reports of the Templeton tracer study of DGMs we were unable to write one on the DGM and nursing because it was a subject that was rarely mentioned by most of the twenty DGMs studied. In the earlier study of DAs[3] they were often dismissive of the DNO, though for some this may have been a reflection of their lack of interest in patient and service issues in general.

Managers' attitudes to nurses are probably due in part to the inadequate ability of many nurses to express their views cogently. Another reason is that nurses are less powerful and less 'difficult' than doctors, so that their views do not compel managers' attention in the way that doctors are able to do. Yet the changes in the supply of nurses and in their education mean that, as Philip Strong and Jane Robinson say at the end of the study 'New Model Management: Griffiths and the NHS':

> 'If few managers have thought much about nursing before, then the time to start thinking is now.'[4]

Shortage of Nurses

This is a major continuing problem in most districts, and is likely to remain so with the decline in the number of school leavers and the growth of better paid and often more attractive career opportunities for young women. There is a gap between the *changed expectations and ambitions* of many young women and the *traditional model of a dedicated nurse*, whose interest in service made her willing to work hard for relatively low pay, in often poor conditions, with unsocial hours, and strict discipline. This gap affects both recruitment and retention. The loss during training (15–20%) plus the 15–20% who fail their exams, and the high annual turnover figure of 30% point to the problems of keeping nurses, even if they are recruited.[5]

A 1987 survey found that there were four major reasons why nurses gave up nursing: too much stress, bad atmosphere at work, excessive workload and a desire for wider experience. These factors were more important than wanting a higher standard of living.[6]

Problems Caused by Reorganisation Since Griffiths

The role of nursing adviser at the district level (DNA) is a new and difficult one, requiring unusual skill to be effective. There have been two main difficulties for those in this role in the early years of the Griffiths reorganisation. One is the lack of any defined authority, the other is the view that it is not a full-time job and should, therefore, be combined with other work. It has either been made a district post combined with another function, such as quality assurance or education and training, or it has been an additional task for the senior nurse in a unit. Both ways of organising district nursing advice have their difficulties: a DNA based at the district may find it hard to exercise leadership because of the greater delegation of power to the units. A unit based DNA has the problem of competition between the units, as well as other problems described below. There are now some signs of a change in approach as some districts have made district appointments with titles like chief nurse or director of nursing as solely nursing posts. These new appointments may meet the need expressed in a study of nursing management in the North West Thames Regional Health Authority, which said that:

> 'there is a strong feeling that a workforce of 2–3000 in each district needs an identifiable leader to set professional standards, values and objectives'.[7]

Like many other new staff jobs it is taking time for the role of DNA to become clearly identified and accepted so that it is clear when advice is needed and whether – and if so, when – the DNA should have authority to issue instructions about how work should be done. This *lack of clarity* is not peculiar to the role of DNA or even to the NHS; one of the long-standing American textbooks, Koontz and O'Donnell, complains about how rare it is for companies to clarify adequately when there should be this authority in a staff job.[8]

The North West Thames study also found that nurses who combined the district advisory role with a post in a unit have special problems. There is the pressure of work and the problem of trying to allocate time between the work for the unit and that for the district advisory role. It can be hard to get a district wide view because the DNA is not usually a member of the district management board and may not have time or be free to attend some of the other relevant meetings.[9]

Lower down, there is concern about nurses being managed by someone who does not have a nursing background and who, it is felt, cannot adequately understand nurses' problems and attitudes. There are problems, too, of *who is responsible for nursing mistakes*, the UGM or the most senior nurse in the unit? Then there are *com-*

munication difficulties that often occur in changed organisations because old loyalties and habits can clash with the requirements of the new organisation. Sometimes, too, extra levels of management have been introduced making communication up and down potentially harder.[10]

Against this recital of difficulties should be set the fact that some nurses enjoy the wider responsibilities that new posts can provide, though few seem to remember that matrons in the past used to have such wider responsibilities!

STEPS TOWARDS THE IDEAL

For Senior Nurse Managers

There are three groups of steps: acting as the leader; influencing nursing practice; and staffing and development.

Acting as the Leader
An important aspect of being a leader is acting as a *role model*, that is as an example to more junior staff both of how to behave and of career possibilities – hence the value for young women of a female role model in a senior job. The value of a role model is true at each level from staff nurse for student nurses up to the most senior manager. Heather-Jane Sears, a hospital manager and one of the young leaders described in Case Study 1 of Chapter 9, illustrated some of the different ways in which a nurse manager can be a role model of good practice. She said:

'I was more of a role model when I was a ward sister than I am now as hospital manager because then I was constantly being watched and teaching.'

but she also illustrated various ways in which she was currently a role model:

'Every time I walk down to a ward I do nursing duties and then I am a role model. For example in lifting a patient, I automatically shift into a professional role model: you are teaching all the time and trying to pull up the standard of excellence in the hospital.'

'I am a role model in a different way from when I was a sister, I am a role model managerially: now I am getting people to examine their practices by showing the value of research-based practice rather than by doing things because we had always done them.'

'I am a role model to my staff about confidentiality, professional attitudes. I talk to patients and their relatives all day and I do that in front of the staff. Interviewing staff, I always have a junior staff nurse there as well for her to learn.'

'I am a role model for time management. As I have to structure my time very carefully and pack a lot into my day, I often talk to the staff about doing the same: about priorities, planning, thinking before you rush in and do. It is very easy on the nursing and domestic side when you are busy to chase your tail.'

If nurses are to be leaders outside their own nursing staff they have to be heard, so learn to *express yourself more cogently* **if you feel that your views do not get sufficient attention.** Take, if necessary in your own time and at your own expense, courses in effective speaking and writing, interdisciplinary negotiating and committee skills and possibly also in assertiveness. Considerable skill is needed, if you are a DNA, to assert yourself diplomatically.

'In presenting your case stick to the issue, do not respond to undercurrents of prejudice towards nurses, or to tensions between the district and units, but work diplomatically towards what you want.' (Advice given by one DNA)

Influencing Nursing Practice
Agree the *overall philosophy* **that should underly all nursing policies and practice.** The DNA with her nursing colleagues can give a lead to nurses by agreeing a nursing philosophy for the district, and by making sure that it is widely known. An example of such a district nursing philosophy is given at the end of this chapter.
     The establishment and maintenance of high standards of care is an essential role of nurse leaders at all levels, but particularly that of ward sister and her equivalents in community care. Those managers who do not have a nursing background will need to enlist the interest and help of their nursing colleagues in doing so. Guidance is available on standards of care and on methods of monitoring them.[11] **A system of regular reporting on performance against measurable standards is**

necessary if attention to quality of care is not to be a number of disconnected and short-lived efforts at improvement.

A high quality of care means not only establishing standards and monitoring that they are being maintained but also looking for ways of *improving* them. A good nursing network will enable you to compare practice as one way of finding what others are doing to improve the standards of care.

Leaders should challenge accepted practice, and encourage their staff to do so too. Nurses are taught to perform, not to ask questions about the output. They need to learn to think *critically* about what they do. It takes time for nurses both to develop the courage to criticise their own practice and to make changes. Unless they are encouraged and supported in doing so, they simply become defensive.

A good example of a new approach to an old problem is Pam Hibbs's research into pressure areas. She found that to prevent pressure sores you must implement a programme of preventive action for particular categories of patients within an hour of their admission to hospital.[12] Pressure sores, in addition to the discomfort to the patient, mean longer in hospital and greater cost to the district. She developed a system for getting data to monitor pressure sores.

Quality of care includes other patient services as well as nursing. The 'hotel' aspects of patient care – catering, cleaning and laundry – are now often grouped with nursing, as they used to be under the old style matron. The task for managers who have these wider duties is to try to ensure that the nursing philosophy is implemented and that the patient is treated like a *customer who has a right to expect good service*. The latter can require a change of attitude that will not happen of its own accord.

See the patient as a customer. Some clinicians, whether nurses or doctors, dislike the idea of patients as customers which they see as alien to their view of professional service. This is understandable. It is a view that can come from the best motives of service and of responsibility to the individual, where the analogy of treating a patient like a relative is seen as more appropriate. However, it is a view that can also come from a feeling of superiority. *If you shy at the word 'customer', ask yourself whether this is because you prefer to think of the patient as dependent upon you?* The idea of a patient as a client or customer with the right both to good service in all its aspects and to be critical of any failings in that service is less comfortable than that of a dependent patient who ought to be grateful.

The 'Patients are People' campaign initiated by Neil Goodwin, the general manager at Central Middlesex Hospital, is one example of different ways of trying to help and encourage staff to provide and contribute to a better service. There are training sessions for managers and staff with the dual purpose of bringing them closer together and of getting them to think of patients as customers who could go elsewhere. There is a monthly Customer Care Award of £50 to anyone who is voted by patients and staff as being the most caring. Staff are encouraged to suggest improvements to service – one should never underrate the ability of staff to notice ways in which service could be improved. The hospital's expertise in promoting caring attitudes is now being sold to other parts of the NHS.[13]

Recognise the patient's right of choice. This ideal applies to both doctors and nurses, whose philosophy towards the patient needs to develop together. One of the merits of the statement of nursing philosophy at the end of this chapter is that in point 8 it stresses the value of ensuring that patients have *choice* rather than being subject to what nurses think is best for them, or what is most convenient for the nurses. Ideally such a value statement should be linked to a companion one by *doctors* in the same Authority.

There are some advantages for nurses as well as for patients in such a recognition, as Catherine McLoughlin, DGM of Haringey Health Authority, pointed out to a group of DGMs when she contrasted the responsibility that patients take – and are expected to take – for themselves before admission to hospital and after their discharge with the dependence on staff while they are in hospital.[14] She said:

> 'I strongly believe that we must change our management of individual care to one which allows them to remain responsible for themselves and the activities which occur to them during their stay in hospital. I believe that is in the individual patient's interest, I also believe that it would reduce the workload being undertaken by nursing staff, therefore, would reduce the stress which they feel.'

Staffing and Development

Recruit and retain nurses. Since nursing shortages are likely to be a continuing and increasing problem, you should actively try to ensure that the units have the nurses that they need. **The relationship between you and junior nurses will be one of the factors that determine how many of the nursing recruits stay, and for how long.** You should ensure that you are known by the nurses, and that you are seen to be *accessible to*, and *supportive of*, them.

Revans showed in the 1960s how much could be learnt by studies of nursing attitudes. However, attitude surveys are useful only if they are followed up. This was the central message of the Revans approach. He wanted hospital staffs to diagnose their own organisational problems and seek to solve them themselves in a more open way than is usual in hospitals.[15]

Use nurses effectively. Ward sisters and other nurse managers should be encouraged to think about the *effective use of their time, and that of their staff* by, for example, comparing staff usage in their own ward with that in other wards.[16] Such comparisons are one of the ways in which the provision of better information can be used to help clinicians, whether doctors or nurses, to compare what they do with their peers as a way of considering the effectiveness with which they work.

Nurses, like other staff, need to be helped and encouraged to *develop themselves*. They – especially the women – may need more encouragement than most to be confident in their abilities and in their aspirations. Encouraging them to acquire additional clinical qualifications is relatively easy, more difficult is the transition from a nurse manager still directly involved in nursing to that of a manager with wider responsibilities. Individuals may need help in deciding whether they really want to make that transition, with the different attitudes that it requires. They will also need training to help them to compete successfully with those from other career backgrounds. **You should encourage them to think positively and proactively about the wider career opportunities now open to them.**

You should seek to *spot leadership talent early*, so that it can be developed. This can be done only if you meet junior nurses in situations where they are not too nervous to speak up. Visiting can provide an opportunity for talking to staff, if you have the skill to do that informally. Sometimes, at least, you should do your homework first by asking managers about their abler staff, and noting who are getting extra qualifications or showing leadership in some way, and then making a point of talking to them. Asking for volunteers for particular projects, like organising an open day, is yet another way of trying to find who are the people who may have promotion potential.

Nurses should be encouraged to develop *specialist knowledge* of particular areas, as Heather-Jane describes in Case Study 1 in Chapter 9. The unit and the district can benefit from having nurses with specialist knowledge, which can range from subjects like child abuse to the prevention of pressure sores. They can lead others in their area of specialist knowledge by highlighting the need for a statement of policy from the Authority, contributing their expertise to discussions of procedures and teaching others to improve their practice.

Help your staff to *learn to express themselves well*, both in speaking and writing.

For General Managers

Recognise that nurse managers have experience that is often relevant to decisions about patient care – for example, care of elderly people. Ensure that they are *included* in such decision-making and, if necessary, help them to make that contribution.

A nursing philosophy like that described at the end of the chapter should be part of the district's planning of services. For example, a principle of not making patients dependent is relevant to decisions about how care should be provided. Raise the question of whether a parallel statement of philosophy should also be drawn up by the doctors working in the Authority.

Do not adopt the popular stereotype of the nurse as the handmaiden of the doctor – for example, *do not overvalue doctors' views compared to nurses'*, nor praise their contribution at the expense of other contributors. You may be tempted to do the latter if you are nervous of doctors' power and are seeking to placate them. **More usually it will be the nurses who need reassurance that you are listening to what they say.**

Review the role of the DNA, perhaps at an away day with your management board, to work out where a district wide nursing view can contribute such as in considering the balance of service for client groups whose care is spread across different units. **Consider the difficulties experienced by the present holder of the job, their causes and what should be done to ensure greater clarification of roles and responsibilities**, for example, the role of the DNA in a complaint involving nursing.

Be alert to the implications of current and projected nurse shortages. Ensure that the problem is being tackled, and *support* those who are doing so.

Consider allocating small sums of money to *encourage* and *reward good care*, as illustrated in the example quoted from Central Middlesex Hospital.

For Chairman and Authority Members

Encourage the senior nurses to develop a statement of the district's nursing philosophy, if they have not already done so, for discussion at the Authority meeting – see the example at the end of this chapter. Seek to ensure that this philosophy is *known* and *understood* by nurses throughout the district.

Discover what figures are provided to other Authorities to check that you are being given **the most appropriate information** for you to judge the standard of care provided in your own district.

Recognise the importance of a *high nursing morale*, and do what you can to show your appreciation of nurses' work.

Consider the ideals listed at the start of the chapter and ask for a statement of nursing objectives, compare them with the suggested ideals to see if there are any **major omissions** that you should query. Ask for an **occasional review of progress** towards the objectives. Similar action should be taken in the new Hospital Trusts.

For Others Concerned With Nursing

Given the anxieties in the nursing profession, there should be a **critical evaluation of the different ways in which nursing leadership is organised**.

SUMMARY

1. Nurses and nursing have not so far received the *critical*, but *supportive*, attention that will be essential in the future.
2. Leadership of, and by, nurses is *wider* than professional leadership. It embraces all aspects of leadership of nurses, whether by nurses or by general managers from other backgrounds. The leadership of nurses must take account of the many *distinctive characteristics* of nursing and of the *changes* affecting nursing.
3. There are *different kinds of ideal* to aim at:

   – the continued and critical attention to *quality of care*;
   – the *effective use* of nurses;
   – high nursing *morale*;
   – effective *training*, *development* and *promotion*;
   – effective *contribution* by nurses to *decisions* about patient care and resource management.

4. Difficulties in achieving the ideal come from the *attitudes of others* towards nurses, *from nurses themselves* and *from* difficulties caused by *reorganisation since the introduction of general management*.

5. Steps towards the ideal suggested for senior nurse managers fall into three groups:

(a) *Acting as the leader:*
    −   act as a role *model*;
    −   *speak up effectively* for nurses, and help your staff to learn to do so too.

(b) *Influencing nursing practice:*
    −   agree *nursing philosophy*;
    −   establish and maintain *high standards of care*;
    −   *challenge* accepted practice and encourage others to do so too;
    −   see the patient as having a *right to good service* in all its aspects;
    −   recognise *patients' right of choice*.

(c) *Staffing and development:*
    −   be active in *recruiting* and *retaining* nurses;
    −   be *accessible to*, and *supportive of*, nurses;
    −   use nurses *effectively*;
    −   help and encourage nurses to *develop themselves*;
    −   encourage a positive approach to *wider career opportunities*.

The suggestions for general managers, for the chairman and authority members are brief enough not to need summarising. Use the account of the ideal as a way of judging what may need attention. The key message is that in the quotation at the head of this chapter: often too little attention is paid to nursing views, in part because many nurses *are not good at expressing themselves*.

A Philosophy of Care for Nursing, Midwifery and Health Visiting in Basingstoke and North Hampshire Health District

Introduction

1. This statement of the beliefs and values that underpin nursing standards in this Health Authority has been compiled by the Nursing Policies and Standards Committee of the Authority (NPSC). It is the first step in the systematic establishment of nursing standards and their use in the evaluation of current nursing practice, its management and development.
2. The approach is consistent with the work of the Quality Assurance and Measurement of Performance Steering Committee of the Authority (QAMOP) and that of the Wessex Regional Nursing Advisory Committee (WRNAC) set out in its paper 'A Regional Framework for Setting Nursing Standards', December 1987.
3. The NPSC will involve as many nurses as possible in developing standards for practice and quality assurance programmes, and collaborate fully with QAMOP and other groups to incorporate multidisciplinary aspects.

Philosophy

It is believed that:
4. Nursing practice is derived from the integration of humane values, and scientific and theoretical knowledge.
Humane values encompass qualities of kindness, concern, compassion, respect for dignity, personal worth, and the autonomy and individuality of each human being together with a reverence for the gift of life.

Scientific and theoretical knowledge, on the other hand, encompasses nursing research and nursing theory, and the sciences relevant to health including physiology, biology, psychology, sociology, demography and epidemiology.

5. The primary goal of nursing practice is to assist people to achieve their optimum level of health.

   If health fails and disability or long-term illness ensue, nursing strives to help the person retain dignity, independence and a sense of worth.

   Nursing has a role in caring for people who are dying; to help them die in peace, comfort and dignity with their final wishes met if possible.

6. Caring is most effective when it is based on individual need. Every person is unique. Nursing must, therefore, provide care which reflects the individuality of the person and takes account of the inter-relatedness of physical, social, psychological and spiritual well-being.

7. Nursing recognises that the needs of patients/clients cannot be separated from the concomitant needs of their families. Nurses must, therefore, work in partnership with patients/clients and other carers. This will involve sharing knowledge and skills, and helping in decision-making about the care to be provided.

8. Nursing has an obligation to offer choice to patients/clients and to uphold their right of self determination. This will entail giving information about alternatives, providing opportunities to ask questions, accepting the patients/clients' right to make and take risks. Further, it entails an advocacy role for nursing when the patients/clients are unable or have impaired ability to make their own decisions.

9. Nurses must collaborate with other professionals and agencies to provide an integrated network of care to patients/clients and carers which is as comprehensive as it can be. Nursing must, therefore, participate fully in developing working relationships which promote proper co-ordination of the management of care.

10. An essential dimension of nursing is to create an environment in which people can explore the implications of changes in their health and be supported in making necessary adjustments.

11. Nurses must keep up with new developments in nursing practice and participate in research to broaden the scope of practice to improve patient/client care.

Glossary

12. Use of the *female* gender has been used when referring to the nurse to ensure consistency.
13. Throughout, the word 'Nurse' includes midwives and health visitors.

1.2.88

4 Leadership and Doctors

'The doctors lead the technology, and therefore the pattern of service. Unless managers get the doctors with them, everything else is just window-dressing. That's where you've got to get change.'
(DGM in the Templeton tracer study)

This chapter is addressed to doctors, and to all those who are in a position to influence doctors.

The DGM quoted above exaggerates – there is a lot else that leaders can usefully do – but by doing so he highlights a *key leadership task*. This is to *enlist doctors' cooperation* in ensuring the provision of effective and efficient health care. It is a task that must not be avoided by those who should be seeking to influence doctors. These include the chairman, general managers and doctors themselves in positions where they have a responsibility for leadership.

THE IDEAL

The ideal attitudes and actions for doctors are listed first, because it is these ideals that leaders, whatever their background, should be seeking to achieve.

Doctors

Doctors will:
1. **Understand the need for management**

(a) Recognise that resources need managing and are always bound to be limited, so that *choices* have to be made about service priorities.
(b) Recognise that resources can be used with varying degrees of effectiveness and be active in considering how to use them *most effectively*.

2. **Be willing to contribute to management**

(a) Realise that if they are not willing to give the time to consider *managerial problems*, and to share in the taking of difficult *resource decisions*, they are leaving this task to managers without medical backgrounds, and may not like the results.

(b) Be willing to serve as *general managers*, *clinical directors* or *programme managers*, though only a few need to be willing.

(c) Elect *representatives* who will work with managers in making choices in service priorities.

3. **Realise the value of learning about management**
4. **Place concern for patient care above professional loyalty**
   So be willing to tackle problems arising from failings in *individual doctors' performance* whatever the cause.
5. **Recognise a corporate responsibility for patient care**
   Hence in bidding for resources accept that others may have a *greater need* for them.
6. **Be active in reviewing their own performance**

(a) Seek to establish *quantitative* and *qualitative* measures of outcomes.

(b) *Compare* their performance with that of their peers and *seek to improve*.

(c) Support those doctors who take the lead in *peer review*.

7. **Show appreciation of the contribution to patient care of nurses, paramedics, and other staff, and behave courteously towards them.**
8. **Recognise and adjust to the changing roles of other professions**, for example, psychologists and biochemists.
9. **Treat patients as intelligent individuals**
   Be *willing to discuss* treatment options and their implications with them.

These ideals do not include the central medical ideals about patient care, because they are about doctors as *members of an organisation*. The last ideal is included because of management's responsibility for ensuring that communication with patients, as the clients, is good.

The ideals described below are those that leaders should pursue and seek to get accepted by all managers whatever their professional background.

Managers

Managers will:

1. **Be resiliently proactive in trying to achieve the ideals listed above**

Avoid the dangers of hand wringing about medical attitudes and of *abdicating any responsibility* for the pursuit of these ideals.

2. **Be seen as the trusted arbitrator between different medical interests**
3. **Express the corporate values and goals in a way that makes sense to doctors**
4. **Seek to create an environment in which professionals can give of their best**
5. **Recognise the stress of doctors' jobs and try to be as helpful as possible**
6. **Seek to ensure that the chairman, general managers and community physicians adopt a common approach in their discussions with doctors**

Doctors and Managers

There is one ideal that should apply to *both* doctors and managers:

Recognise and understand the different roles that doctors and managers have to play in the NHS and the attitudes that come both from that and from differences in training

Chairmen

The chairman will

1. **Recognise that the chairman's status helps in negotiations with doctors and therefore be willing to devote the necessary time.**
2. **Be supportive of, and available to, doctors' representatives and listen to their concerns but recognise that their arguments may be one-sided.**
3. **Take care really to understand the issue that is arousing doctors' ire, so as not to make injudicious comments.**
4. **Agree – and keep to – the strategy for pursuing changes that move nearer to the ideal.**

DIFFICULTIES IN REACHING THE IDEAL[1]

The Introduction to Part II gave five possible reasons for the difficulties that leaders may have in seeking to influence others: differences in roles, differences in training and experience, competition for scarce resources, differences in relative power, and particular personality problems. All are reasons why the relationship between doctors and managers so often causes problems for the managers.

Differences in Role

Doctors' primary role is to *treat individual patients*. They may play other roles as well: teaching, researching, fund raising, acting as a medical representative in discussions with management, managing their department or firm, and serving on national medical councils. But in their primary role, their responsibility is to the individual patient and not to the organisation. They will want – indeed have – an obligation to do the best that they can for their patient. An important organisational consequence of the pursuit of this role is that they *use current resources* of the organisation, and take actions that *mortgage future resources*.

Doctors may learn something of management in some of their other roles, but in their primary one it is their professional relationship to the patient rather than responsibility to the organisation that employs them that is paramount. They will try to get the resources that they think are necessary, often without considering the *wider implications* of doing so. Unless they have to ask for more resources, they may not consider the future resource implications of their actions. They may be unwilling to recognise resource constraints, like the small number of medical staff committees who passed motions in 1988 saying that they saw no alternative but a significant overspend.

General managers are responsible for maintaining expenditure within budget and ensuring that the service priorities are adhered to. These responsibilities can be threatened by consultants' actions. The role that managers are employed to perform means that they are likely to be viewed with suspicion by doctors, who see them as interfering with their own role of serving the patient. This suspicion is aggravated if the manager seeks to restrict their *access to resources* or to ensure that doctors' contracts are fulfilled. Changes in financing proposed in *Working with Patients* will reduce one cause of friction.

Differences in Training and Experience

The relationship between doctors and non-medical managers is made more difficult by differences in their training and careers. Doctors' lengthy and arduous training produces a group with its *own culture* and sense of belonging to an *elite clan*. This is reinforced in those coming from a medical family. Doctors are trained to think *individualistically* rather than organisationally; to have a loyalty to medical ethics but not to the organisation that employs them; to pursue their individual goals rather than to consider wider goals, including the *needs of their colleagues*.

Doctors take the lead in the patient's treatment and grow accustomed to being in command of other services to the patient. They are used to *deference* from most of those with whom they come in contact: patients, nurses, paramedics and – if they are consultants – from junior doctors. This can breed arrogance and a dismissal of what they may still insist on calling, 'administrators', perhaps because they dislike the connotation of 'managers'. At its worst, this arrogance can result in an attitude that is unwilling to consider either the *effectiveness* of their own performance or its *repercussions* on others. Because of their powerful position, it is much easier for consultants than for other employees in the NHS to behave with little regard for the difficulties that their attitudes and actions cause for others.

Doctors' work is stressful, as figures for alcoholism and suicides amongst doctors show. Perhaps because of this, they may work on a short fuse and lose their temper more commonly than do other members of staff; they say what they think of others more readily than is usual amongst managers, or even other professional people. The stress under which they work is one of the explanations, as we are all liable to be more irritable when stressed. A further explanation is that because of their powerful position and individualistic role they have had *fewer constraints upon their behaviour* than is common in organisational life.

Managers learn different skills and attitudes. They learn, even if they came from a clinical background, to think about their work as part of a *larger organisation*, which means that they have to cooperate with others, to coordinate their work and that of their department with the work of other departments. They owe a loyalty to the organisation and are expected to achieve the objectives set by their superior, the Authority and the centre.

Managers' success will largely depend upon their ability to *influence others*, often those over whom they have little or no control and whose work – if they are in charge of people with a different training from their own – they may not fully understand. Doctors can more easily rely upon their professional expertise as the basis for exercising authority; managers must develop *interpersonal skills*, a capacity to understand the other person's point of view and to think politically about ways of effecting change. They should learn to be diplomatic in their approach to sensitive problems, and skilful in their capacity to *motivate* the different personalities who work for them. They will often need considerable *perseverance* and *resilience* if they are to effect change.

Doctors and managers, therefore, have different – and *potentially conflicting* – roles to play. This makes them look at problems differently. The fact that their training and careers have given them distinctive attitudes, skills and habits of relating to other people makes it even harder for them to understand each other. Managers' training and experience should make it easier for them to bridge the gap of understanding, and to express themselves in language that helps to do so.

Competition for Scarce Resources

The potential for conflict between doctors and managers – *and between doctors themselves* in competing for resources – has become greater with more financial pressure upon the NHS. This has been exacerbated by the attempts to give greater priority to non-acute services, when most of the doctors work in the acute services. Managers have had to take unpopular actions to try to balance the books, and to ensure that resources are distributed in accordance with national priorities for patient care.

Differences in Relative Power

Doctors' powerful position has always posed problems for managers – and for politicians and members, too – in seeking to make changes that affect doctors. Doctors' fears that general management will affect their power – and, most importantly, their clinical autonomy – has increased their suspicions of managerial intentions.

Personality Clashes

The intensity of personality clashes that sometimes exists between doctors working in the same hospital is one of the distinctively difficult problems for those responsible for ensuring the provision of good patient care. There are probably two reasons why these personality clashes are a particular problem amongst doctors. One is the fact that doctors tend to stay in the same district once they become consultants so that personal feuds can go on for a long time. Another is that doctors have had less need to *learn to accommodate* to other people.

STEPS TOWARDS THE IDEAL

These are about what the individual leader can do, and not about possible institutional changes. Stating the ideal shows *what to aim at*; you should, as in other chapters, *adapt* the ideal to your own views and situation. Since attempting to lead doctors is difficult, and can often be discouraging, it is particularly important to have a *clear picture* of your ideal as stimulus, guide and encouragement. Understanding the nature of the difficulties that can stand in the way of reaching the ideal, and the reasons for them, are also essential steps towards knowing what to do. The first task is:

Bridging the Management/Medical Divide

'Bridging' is the right word, because one would not want there to be no divide, as the NHSTA booklet on doctors says:

> 'a measure of disagreement and conflict between managers and doctors over key issues can actually be good for the Service, in that it subjects such issues to scrutiny from more than one perspective'.[2]

It is desirable that problems should be examined both from the *managerial perspective* of optimising resources and considering priorities, and from the *clinical perspective* of doing the best for the individual patient. It is the suspicion of, and misunderstandings about, each other's motives that need to be overcome. A key task for managers is to show doctors that they are *also committed to patient care*, but that this commitment necessarily takes a different form. For doctors the task is to understand the *necessity for*, and the *nature of*, management and what its concepts and techniques can offer.

Managers must recognise the very real fears that many doctors have about managerial actions; as Dr McQuillan says:

> 'Their fear that clinical freedom will be eroded by managers is still one of the most powerful factors motivating doctors to resist changes proposed by managers to ensure the most effective use of

resources. This fear is not confined to older established doctors, but is also shared by those in training.'[3]

There needs to be a growth of general understanding which is best fostered by *personal contact*, both within the hospital or district and at meetings outside. An example of the latter were the meetings for general managers and leading medics on new medical developments held soon after the introduction of general management; general managers said that they found these helpful in understanding medical attitudes, as well as for the specific subjects discussed.

There also needs to be a common understanding of specific issues. Both doctors and managers must realise that it is important to *keep each other informed* of likely changes and to do so at an early stage so that the possible repercussions can be explored. As one of the DGMs in the Templeton study said:

'I can't stress too much how important it is to be able to drop in and chat to consultants in a relaxed way. Where I've not done that, thinking perhaps that the issue was sufficiently straightforward or that I didn't have time, it's nearly always come unstuck or had a rough passage.'

Encouraging Doctors to Take on Managerial Roles

This can have a number of advantages. It can bring both a medical perspective to managerial problems and a responsibility for problem resolution. It can help to bridge the medical–management divide. It may be somewhat easier for doctors to manage other doctors, since their credibility for understanding the problems that doctors face should be higher. 'May be' because, at the time of writing, there had been no study of how medical UGMs compare with UGMs from other backgrounds. One problem that many face is that they come to a senior management post without experience in more junior ones. The difficulties of doing this may be one of the reasons why a number have returned to full-time work as consultants.

Some general managers have been successful in encouraging doctors to take on different kinds of managerial jobs. Clinical directors, for example, have been appointed in a number of hospitals. An article in *The Lancet* described the good results achieved in resource management at Guy's, where thirteen clinical directorates were appointed. The proposals in *Working with Patients* should encourage more doctors to be involved in management.

Providing Management Training for Doctors

The National Health Service Training Authority's 1988 policy proposals on 'Doctors and Management Development' seeks to clarify what should be done, and by whom. It suggests that the main purpose of management development for doctors should be to:

1. help clinicians enhance their management skills so as to improve clinical practice;
2. develop the managerial skills of doctors with Head of Department responsibility;
3. support doctors in representative or elected roles; and
4. support those doctors who are making the transition into a management career.[5]

The paper emphasises that management skills are an integral part of a doctor's professional practice so that it is wrong to distinguish clinical practice from management. The NHSTA policy statement is diplomatic. The four purposes listed above are useful aims, but development should also encourage a change in attitudes. Hence we should list two further aims:

5. help doctors to recognise that *resources have to be managed*, and that if they do not do so someone else will have to;
6. persuade doctors who take on managerial roles that there is a *body of knowledge and skills that it would help them to learn* and that the authoritarian approach, which is traditional in much medical practice, will often antagonise those with whom they will have to work.

Developing Information Systems for Doctors to use

The Resource Management Initiative launched in 1986 is still at the time of writing in the early stages of assessment, but if it works well it can encourage a different approach by doctors to the use of resources. We do not know yet whether the attitude expressed by Peter Wright, one of the consultants at a pilot site (the Freeman Hospital in Newcastle-upon-Tyne) is shared by other participating consultants or is going to grow in other districts. He said:

'we recognise that we have a responsibility to use resources well and we want to run it and be in control. If we don't, someone else will do it for us in a way that will probably be bad news.'[6]

Using the General Methods of Change Management

These methods, which were briefly discussed on p. 22, are relevant to any leader who is seeking to effect change. They are particularly important for leaders in their relations with doctors because of the difficulties posed by the unusual combination of strong individualism with clannish support if one of their number is seen to be threatened by an outsider – that is, someone who does not belong to the medical clan. Even medical general managers may be seen as having 'changed sides'.

Where the proposed change is likely to be unpopular with doctors, remember that the first stage of the change process is *'unfreezing' attitudes*. Be on the lookout for events that may encourage unfreezing, when doctors may be more understanding of the need for change, and hence more willing to accept it. Such opportunities may come, for example, from an unfavourable report on an aspect of the district's medical care, or from a major financial crisis.

Develop your strategy for achieving change: agree what you are aiming at with those whose support you need, then plan how you can overcome doctors' potentially powerful antagonism to change. There are three steps:

1. **Discover who matters**

(a) Who are the *opinion leaders*?
(b) Who are *potential allies*, and who will at least be neutral?
(c) Who are, or could be, *dangerous opponents*?
(d) Who are good sources of *information* about medical reactions?
(e) Who would be good at *contributing to management*?

2. **Understand leading individuals**
     Study the leading doctors: what *matters most* to them; what are their *concerns*; what *upsets* them; and what *skills* could they contribute to resolving a problem or pushing forward a change?

3. **Enlist support**

(a) Show understanding of the situation that doctors (especially leading doctors) are dealing with – this may require prior work on your part – and seek to *build goodwill* by trying to help with their problems.

(b) Gain doctors' respect by providing an efficient service for them.

(c) Get doctors interested in solving a problem by asking for their help or *giving the problem to them to solve* – an old ploy, but one that can work particularly well with doctors because they are intelligent, are used to and enjoy problem solving and may like to demonstrate their superior ability.

(d) *Use the right language* in talking with doctors: talk about 'improving the organisation of patient care' rather than using management words like 'efficiency' that can grate on medical ears.

(e) Finally, show you are *trustworthy*. This may seem to go against the machiavellian advice that is implicit in some of the points above, especially 'discover who matters', but political calculation is not incompatible with trustworthiness in the sense of keeping to one's word. That is vital because trust once lost is hard, often impossible, to regain, as John Harvey-Jones points out:

> 'Trust, once it begins to deteriorate, quite suddenly flips over and becomes a sort of galloping corrosion of suspicion which is very difficult to halt. Trust is tremendously difficult to build up and all too easy to destroy, so it is worth taking all sorts of actions, even if they appear to be finicky, to avoid losing it.'[7]

This is useful advice in all relationships, but it is of utmost importance to the relationship between managers and doctors because the danger of doctors being suspicious of managers' actions, even if they are doctors themselves, is greater than in most, perhaps all other, relationships.

Leading doctors to recognise managerial problems and to be willing to help to solve them is one of the most difficult leadership tasks for chairmen, general managers, RMOs and DMOs. It requires vision, courage, persistence, understanding and skill. It is to be hoped that more doctors who have the skill, or the ability to acquire it, will take up this challenging leadership task and seek to achieve the ideals suggested earlier.

SUMMARY

1. If you are in a position to influence doctors, you have a key

leadership task. The *doctors'* ideals to be pursued are that the doctors will:

(a) understand the *need* for management;
(b) be willing to *contribute* to management;
(c) realise the value of *learning about management*;
(d) place concern for *patient care* above professional loyalty;
(e) recognise that *others' need* for more resources may be greater than theirs;
(f) be active in *reviewing their own performance*;
(g) show *appreciation of the contribution of others* to patient care;
(h) recognise and adjust to the changing roles of *other professions*;
(i) treat patients as *intelligent individuals*.

2. The ideals for *your own behaviour in seeking to lead doctors* is that you will:

(a) be *resiliently proactive* in trying to achieve the ideals listed above;
(b) be seen as the *trusted arbitrator* between different medical interests;
(c) express the corporate values and goals in a way that *makes sense to doctors*;
(d) provide an *efficient and sympathetic service* to doctors, so that they can give of their best;
(e) agree a *common approach* to changes that affect doctors with all those necessarily involved.

An ideal that should be common to both doctors and managers who are not doctors is that they will recognise and seek to understand each other's *different viewpoints*.

3. *The major difficulties in reaching the ideal* stem from differences in the role of doctors and managers, so that they see problems differently. For managers who are not doctors, this is accentuated by differences in their training and experience. Doctors' powerful position makes it hard to get changes accepted that *they do not see as beneficial*.

4. *The main steps that you should take towards achieving the ideal*, whatever your professional background, are:

(a) seek to foster *mutual understanding*;
(b) encourage doctors to *take on managerial roles*; or if you are a doctor, consider doing so;
(c) provide *management training* for doctors; and if you are a doctor, accept the need for such training;

(d) develop *information systems* that are useful to doctors;
(e) recognise the difficulties of implementing change and apply the *guidelines for managing change*:

- identify whose opinions are *most important* to achieving a particular change;
- seek to understand their motivation;
- present the change in *language* that is acceptable to doctors;
- *enlist support*.

(f) Above all, show that you are *trustworthy*.

5 Sharing the Leadership

'It is remarkable how well you and the DGM gell, so that you each come in as appropriate.' (An observer of a meeting commenting to the chairman)

This chapter is about the different ways and relationships in which leadership needs to be, or can be, *shared*. It starts with a discussion of the most important and the only inescapable example of leadership sharing in the NHS – that between a chairman and general manager. It is this relationship that will be analysed in the usual three parts: ideal, difficulties, and steps towards the ideal. Then there will be a more general account of the nature and value of leadership sharing in other relationships.

A special aspect of being a leader at the top of some organisations is that the leadership has to be shared. The most common form of sharing is, as in the NHS, between the chairman and the chief executive. In each region and district there is this shared leadership role, as there will be in the Hospital Trusts. Prescribed leadership sharing as between the chairman and the general manager is uncommon. More common is *informal* sharing of leadership, so the account of this at the end of the chapter will be relevant to many more readers.

THE IDEAL

The leadership role is necessarily shared between the chairman and the general manager, though the *extent* to which it is shared, and *how* it is shared, will vary. **The ideal is that this sharing should be complementary, so that the two together achieve more than they could do independently.** They should make the best use of each other's *different roles*, and of their *relative strengths*.

There are both demand and choice aspects of the leadership role in the chairman's and general manager's jobs. The chairman is the *figurehead* for the district, and should play that aspect of the leadership role on public occasions, particularly where the policies of the DHA are under attack. He or she as the chairman of the DHA should also be its leader. The general manager should *lead the staff of the district*, and particularly the senior managers, and the chairman should do nothing to undermine that leadership by being seen as a way of bypassing the general manager. These are the roles that each should play, that is the 'demand' part of each job. There is also often a choice as to how they share the job of leading the district.

The ideal is a partnership: the two should work in tandem on major changes and negotiations. Yet the chairman needs to retain a *visible independence* of the managers, so as not to be seen as the managers' mouthpiece.

The time that the chairman gives to the district or region obviously affects what can be done. The ideal is that the chairman gives more than the minimum time that is required to perform the demand aspects of the role, so that other leadership tasks, that are not exclusively the general manager's, can best be shared according to knowledge, experience and personality.

General managers often find their jobs to be lonely ones, particularly in times of difficulty. **Ideally both DGMs and RGMs should be able to use their chairman as a person that they can turn to for advice, help and support.**

Ideally, too, the chairman should, like any other boss, be concerned about, and seek to assist the development of, their general manager.

WHY EFFECTIVE SHARING CAN BE DIFFICULT TO ACHIEVE

The difficulties for both chairman and general manager come from accommodating their own leadership role to that played by the other. The difficulties are usually greater for the general manager because chairmen are in a stronger position to determine how they want to play the role. The *potential difficulties*, as described by the DGMs who were part of the Templeton tracer study of DGMs,[1] are as follows:

1. **The time that the chairman gives to the job.** This may be too little – a day a week or less – to act as a leader except in meetings of the DHA. The general manager may then feel that the chairman's leadership and support is not available when required, particularly on difficult public occasions. Alternatively the chairman may work almost or wholly full-time, then the general manager's difficulty may be that the chairman wants to do *too*

much, thus infringing on what the general manager sees to be his own role.

2. **The chairman's inadequate knowledge of the NHS.** A chairman with no previous knowledge can take a lot of the general manager's time during the induction period. The general manager may also be anxious about the chairman saying the wrong thing in public or in difficult negotiations.

3. **The chairman's view of the role may differ from that which the general manager thinks is correct.** Taking the lead where the general manager thinks it inappropriate, for example, or failing to do so when the general manager thinks the chairman should.

4. **General managers will commonly be concerned if they think that the chairman is undermining their position in some way.** This can be either by supporting members of their own staff against them, or by taking a different stance in Authority meetings from that indicated in prior discussions.

5. **A chairman who is unable or unwilling to lead the Authority discussions.** Such a chairman will also cause the general manager difficulty. The chairman may be unable to lead the Authority because he or she lacks the political skills to guide the discussion. The chairman may be unwilling to do so, believing that his or her task is to ensure that the subjects are well discussed and not to steer the discussion towards the conclusions desired by the managers even if they were agreed at a briefing meeting.

Chairmen have the problem of learning to understand both their own role, and the strengths and weaknesses of the general manager. They may need to learn what role they want to play, and how this best fits with that played by the general manager. They may think that their general manager should be playing a stronger leadership role, and be concerned about how to get him to do so. Another of their difficulties may be reconciling the role that the regional chairman wants them to play with the expectations of their members and of the general manager.

STEPS TOWARDS THE IDEAL

The relationship between the chairman and the general manager resembles that of a marriage. It has some of the same difficulties, and needs some of the same insights and tact. Both partners have to *learn to work together* and to evolve the *particular roles* that each plays. In a marriage, the division of roles and of tasks is more fluid because nowadays there is no clear guide as to who does what in the house or outside it; the roles of chairman and of general manager are more defined, but even so there can be great variation in practice as the Templeton tracer study of DGMs showed.

Both need to learn to understand each other's *strengths and weaknesses*, and to establish a sufficiently close relationship that they can discuss how they can make best use of their partnership. They should agree on their *strategy in negotiations* with the region and other bodies and in handling problems that have aroused – or are likely to arouse – controversy in the district. They also need to agree on the *role* that they are each going to play in negotiations and public meetings.

There are also *specific steps* that each should take to achieve the ideal, and these are now described separately.

Chairmen

Chairmen should ask themselves: 'what can I most usefully contribute in my particular district, apart from the work that I must do?'

1. **The prime role is to lead the DHA.** Doing that effectively requires a good understanding of the issues to be discussed, an understanding of the different viewpoints amongst the members, and of their likely reactions. This means both ensuring that the managers provide good briefing and having other sources of information as well.
2. **There is an important role in providing a more detached view of problems, and often a wider experience than the DGM and other senior managers can have.** The chairman should ensure that the DGM and senior managers think through the philosophy underlying district policies.
3. **The chairman has a leadership role on public occasions.** This is particularly the case when the Authority is under attack.
4. **The chairman may need to encourage the DGM to act more like a leader.** How necessary this is will depend upon the DGM's personality and background. **A few chairmen may need to do the opposite, to restrain the DGM from taking too forceful a lead**

when that may be bad tactics, or to give senior managers more headroom.

5. **The chairman has potentially a very important role in stimulating the general manager to learn to be a more effective manager.** It is all too easy for senior managers to think that by the time they have reached a top job they have nothing more they need to learn about managing.

6. **Some at least of the leading consultants will want to have discussions with the chairman, as the top person in the district.** They will want to make sure that their views are known and understood.

7. **Recognition of the good work done by other staff – especially by nurses**, as the most numerous staff and those who are in particularly stressful jobs. This is an important potential part of the chairman's role as figurehead for the district. Attending staff occasions like prize giving can help to show recognition of good work.

There are many other ways in which the chairman could usefully take a lead, particularly if the DGM is not doing so. Reading through the ideal in the previous chapters should provide a checklist for thinking about what needs more attention in the district, and whether this can be done without sacrificing some work that is even more important. The chairman may, for example, need to ensure that the DGM and other senior managers adequately *clarify their objectives*, though that ought to be the DGM's task. There may be a need, too, to ensure that more is done to get *community views and real feedback* about patient views. To give a different kind of example, a chairman with good external contacts can be a source of information about what is happening in the local community and outside the district and seek, if necessary, to *broaden the knowledge and interests* of the DGM and other senior managers. A skilful, politically knowledgeable chairman can also take the lead in relations with MPs and in some regional negotiations. **The division of leadership should depend very much upon the relative skills, knowledge and interests of the chairman and DGM.**

RGM or DGM

Part of the skill of being a general manager is establishing a *productive relationship with the chairman*, making the best use of the time and abilities that he or she can contribute. It should be possible to do so with most chairmen, even if difficult and egocentric, provided you are able to look at them unemotionally and recognise what are the best ways to influence them.

1. **Consider what the chairman wants from the job, and try to provide it**: some, for example, may enjoy public recognition by taking part in public occasions.

2. **Do not underrate what the chairman can contribute**, as a number of the DGMs in the Templeton study seemed to do. Get to understand the strengths and weaknesses of the chairman in comparison with your own and **try to use the chairman to achieve the overall ideal** stated at the start of the chapter. Take a positive view of what the chairman can contribute rather than overrating the importance of what you do, or deploring what you do not like about your chairman.

3. Use your chairman, if possible, **as a way of learning about what is happening in the community,** or outside it.

4. **Seek to enhance the chairman's credibility in the district**: for example, try to present the chairman's demands on other staff in a positive light, such as saying that they come from an interest in patient care.

5. **Make the best use of your time with chairmen who have little time to spend in the district** by arranging meetings well in advance, and making sure that briefings are succinct and informative.

6. Make sure that the chairman is **adequately briefed about problems in the district**, and for any public meeting.

7. Recognise the value that staff in general, and consultants in particular, can place on having contact with the chairman and, if necessary **help the chairman to understand how to relate to consultants without undermining general management**.

OTHER FORMS OF LEADERSHIP SHARING

The relationship between chairman and general manager is a form of leadership sharing that is inherent in their roles although there are important choices in how it is exercised. The relationship between a manager and the deputy manager has no essential continuing role sharing as the deputy may deputise only in the manager's absence.

However, a deputy role more than that of other subordinates offers the manager *choices* in what the deputy is asked to do.

Using Your Subordinates' Qualities

Managers can – and should – use their subordinates to take the lead in areas *where they personally are weak*, or where they judge that their subordinate can *more easily accomplish the aim*. For example, there are choices to be made in the relative roles to be played by the DGM and the DMO in discussions with consultants. A manager whose temperament is to concentrate on the work to be done and on driving it forward can use a more 'people oriented' subordinate, who may nor may not be the deputy, to be more considerate of people's feelings and to provide feedback about their reactions. Managers can also usefully *share the leadership* with their subordinates on occasions as Peter, the DGM in Case Study 4 describes on p. 148.

Leadership Sharing in a Group

Leadership sharing also takes place *within a group*. Next time you are in a working group, observe what is happening. You will notice that *different people take the lead at different times* because they are able to make different types of contribution. Often you may observe the same people playing a similar role in another group. The roles you may most easily observe are: focusing members on the task to be done; summing up; seeking to smooth any personality clashes; and contributing a new idea that changes the subject of the discussion.

If you are putting together a project team, it is worth thinking about the contributions that people will make not just in terms of their jobs but also of their *personality* – Belbin's book on *Management Teams* is a useful guide to the different roles that need to be played and to what happens if you get the mix wrong.[2] You may say: 'that is all very well if one has the luxury of choosing who should be the members of a working group, but I have to work in groups where there is no choice'. Even then, Belbin's analysis can be of help because he says that individuals may prefer one role, but can play another. You can usefully therefore ask yourself what may be missing to make a group work more effectively. If you notice that the group is ineffective in particular ways – such as failing to reach decisions, or being very limited in its ideas – then ask yourself whether you can supply the missing ingredient ('particular team role', in Belbin's language), or if not whether there is another member of the group who has the ability, and whom you can encourage, to do so.

Complementary Leadership Skills

The overall lesson for any manager – but particularly a senior one – is that there are different aspects of leadership and that these often will – and should be – shared. This is reassuring because it means that you *do not have to be good at everything*, indeed you will not have the ability – or the time – to be that. What you do need is an ability to recognise your own strengths and weaknesses and those of the people with whom you work, and the leadership ability to get them to *complement you*. This is most important in the relationship between general manager and the chairman, but it is true of other relationships too. Look amongst your subordinates, and perhaps your colleagues, for people who can complement you, and encourage them to lead in areas where you are weak either in knowledge or personality. When you are working in a group remember that group leadership is not a single task performed by one person, but that different forms of leadership are required even though one person is in the chair.

SUMMARY

1. A few jobs require *leadership to be shared*. In the NHS this is true for the relationship between the chairman and the general manager. More common is the *informal sharing of leadership* that takes place in groups and sometimes in other relationships.
2. The ideal relationship between chairman and RGMs or DGMs is a *complementary one* that enables them jointly to contribute more to the district than they could do independently. The ideal is a partnership that makes the best use of the differences in their roles and in their abilities and experience.
3. Difficulties in achieving the ideal can come from either personality not accommodating to the leadership role played by the other. Difficulties will come, too, if the chairman *usurps* part of the general manager's role or fails to provide support and guidance. Similarly the general manager may not make good use of the chairman, nor provide good briefing on issues.
4. In achieving the ideal, there needs to be some of the same

insights and tact that characterise successful marriages. Both partners need to learn to understand each other's strengths and weaknesses. Chairmen should develop the general manager's leadership abilities. They should also use their status where it will help in negotiations and to show appreciation of good work. Part of the skill of being an effective general manager is establishing a productive relationship with the chairman.

5. The fact that leadership can be shared at times in other relationships extends what you can achieve as a leader. Look for those who can *complement* you where you are weak, and encourage them to take the lead there.

6. There is also leadership sharing in groups. Recognise the *different leadership roles there are to be played in an effective group*, and take these into account in forming a project group.

This chapter mainly discussed how the Authority chairman and general manager can most effectively share their leadership role, but the same lessons will apply to the chairman and general manager of a Hospital Trust.

6 Leadership and the District Health Authority

'. . . *our findings suggest that the DHA, informally or even just by its very existence, exerts considerable influence.*' (Templeton Series on District General Managers, Issue Study No. 3)[1]

The influence the DHA exerted upon district general management, shown by the Templeton tracer study of DGMs, was true for the DHA then despite the ambiguities of its role. The new form of DHA proposed in the 1989 White Paper, '*Working for Patients*',[2] should be in a position to exercise more influence upon managerial decisions. Hence effective leadership in the Authority will be even more important than before. This does not just mean leadership by the chairman, important though that will be. Others, especially the DGM, can and should also contribute to the leadership that will be needed to achieve the ideals. The non-executive members may also, at times, need to provide leadership.

Chairmen are constrained in a variety of ways in their leadership of the DHA including: the time that they give to the job, their understanding of the issues, the attitudes of the members to the leadership, and the role played by the DGM. All of these constraints chairmen can seek to change, but their role in the new form of DHA will still be a difficult one.

Clearly the new DHAs will be very different from the old ones, but there are still valuable lessons to be learnt from the experience of those who sought to make the old DHAs more effective. Therefore, this chapter draws upon that experience.

One of the important changes in the form of DHA proposed in *Working for Patients* is the inclusion of up to five executive and five non-executive members. This introduces a new relationship into the working of the DHA.

The rationale for the new DHAs may be seen primarily, or even solely, in managerial terms so that they resemble a board of directors that includes non-executive directors, who are appointed to contribute an outside perspective and to provide knowledge and skills that differ from those of the executive members. However, the non-executive members of the DHA must do more than that because the

DHA necessarily has to consider, and to decide between, the needs of different kinds of patients, within national policies, and to make decisions that can arouse strong feelings locally. This chapter is, therefore, based on the assumption that an important reason for the new DHAs, as for their predecessors, will be to provide for *local influence* on decisions about health care provision and *for public accountability* in their district. Such decisions are, of course, subject to the demands and constraints of national priorities.

THE IDEAL

The major overall ideal is that the chairman, DGM and other members should share common values, trust each other, and jointly seek to use the DHA to contribute to the provision of the best possible care, taking account of local interests and needs, within national policies and the resources available.

In addition to their new task of buying the best services that they can afford while continuing to manage at least some services, the new DHAs should ideally:

1. **Act as the voice of the community in discussing managerial policies and actions**, Kenneth Clarke's remarks to the 1986 NAHA annual general meeting should still apply.

   'There are three areas in which members need to respond to the voice of the community they serve – informing themselves about public expectations, informing the public about the service locally and finally accounting to the public for the service provided.'[3]

2. **Judge the relative priority of the demands made by the different interest groups in the community within the framework of national policies.**

3. **Define and monitor the standard of care provided within the district.** This, and the previous ideal become more important responsibilities in the new DHAs.

4. **Seek to enhance the morale of staff working in the district by showing appreciation of good performance.** This role will also be important for members of the boards of Hospital Trusts. Indeed, where most of the NHS staff in a district work in such trusts it will be more important for Trust members than for DHA members.

Other ideals relate to shared leadership problems:

1. **The non-executive members distance themselves from the managers so that they are able to contribute an outside perspective and to ensure that patient needs are never forgotten**.
2. **The executive members accept that the DHA has a useful role to play and do their best to help non-executive members to contribute effectively**. They recognise the value of having their priorities for care questioned, and the assumptions underlying their recommendations challenged, particularly if it is done constructively, and realise that there is a danger of public servants thinking that they always know best what is good for the public.
3. **Members' time is used efficiently and they get the information that they need**.
4. **Members accept that the district is a part of a national service with the constraints that that imposes, and that they will have to take hard decisions about priorities**.

DIFFICULTIES IN ACHIEVING THE IDEAL

Working for Patients suggests that the proposed change in membership will overcome the 'long-standing lack of clarity about the role of health authorities', and provide 'a single focus for effective decision-making'.[4] Yet in a Service where decisions can arouse such strong emotions there are likely to be differences amongst both the executive and non-executive members. Even if all involved are agreed about the role of the DHA there will still be the problem of achieving a good balance between observing *national priorities* and satisfying *local needs*. This may become more difficult in the new DHAs since the non-executive members may not be as sensitive to, or as interested in, local views as previous members. Nor can it be assumed that the CHCs will find it as easy to take over that part of the DHA's role as *Working for Patients* implies.

Other difficulties that arose in DHAs in the past may still be a problem in some of the new DHAs, namely:

1. **Some managers may think that the DHA is, and should be, only a rubber stamp** on decisions of the district management board.
2. **Getting sufficient able non-executive members who can give enough time to the work**.
3. **Turnover in membership** which makes consistency of policies and

the development of members' knowledge and contribution more difficult.

4. **The inability of members adequately to digest the information provided and to understand the complexity of some of the issues involved, particularly in limited time**.

5. **The danger that members will underestimate the effort required to prepare themselves for their responsibilities**, both in understanding current health issues and in acquiring detailed local knowledge of the district services for which they are responsible and for which they contract.

6. **Problems arising from the mismatch that can exist between what is good for patients and what is good for staff**, which may be highlighted by members' role of monitoring patient care. As Charlotte Williamson, Vice-Chairman of the York Health Authority, pointed out:

> 'Changes made towards better non-clinical care for patients are often made at a cost to staff. More choice and control for patients can mean less choice and control for staff. More autonomy for patients can mean less emotional dependency on staff, as well as less compliant behaviour towards them.'[5]

She defined non-clinical care as that affecting patients' *psychological* or *social* welfare.

STEPS TOWARDS THE IDEAL

It should be remembered that DHAs are likely to exercise more influence than managers may be willing to credit, as the Templeton tracer study of DGMs said:

> 'DHA meetings give the impression, when we observe them, that they result in very few shifts in policy. But that does not necessarily make them the rubber stamps they are sometimes accused of being. Most DGMs assess what is likely to be acceptable to the DHA from a very early stage of all policy making. The DHA is always there in the background as a conglomerate of local pressures that sets strong limits around what the manager can seek to change . . . the actual meeting may be almost a formality, but only because by their views – or rather the potential views attributed to them – the members play a major role, either in early informal discussions or as a tacit and unseen, internalised presence.'[6]

The new DHAs should be able to exercise more influence, so it is even more important that the ideals should be realised. A lot of work was done to try and improve the working of DHAs. Both Chris Ham and Stuart Haywood[7] worked with interested authorities on trying to define and improve the role played by the DHA. Their experience, that of the Templeton tracer studies, discussions with other DGMs and the 1986 NAHA report of a working party on the appointment, training and work of DHA members[8] can all suggest some useful steps for the new Authorities too:

1. **Clarify what the DHA should be discussing**. This needs to be done concretely rather than in abstract terms.

2. **Plan the agenda ahead**. The agenda should include both regular reviews of performance and agreed subjects to be considered at particular meetings together with space for discussing unexpected subjects of concern. A very few subjects should also be selected for special attention in the next year.

3. **Ensure that there are opportunities for discussion on selected key problems before papers are presented to a formal meeting of the DHA**. Such discussions may take place in a joint working party, in a seminar, in regular sub-committees or in informal meetings before the DHA. Whatever method is used should provide for 'meaningful debate and discussion'[9] between members and managers.

4. **Agree what information is required by the DHA and make it as digestible and informative as possible**. Specifically, review what performance standards have been set and what monitoring information is provided to check on their achievement. Members should satisfy themselves that the standards of non-clinical care, as defined above by Charlotte Williamson, are high. This should be one of the purposes of their visits to district facilities.

5. **The chairman, the DGM and the non-executive members themselves should seek to make the best use of the latters' individual abilities** within the constraints of the time that each can give. The Brunel study[10] notes two main types of member: those who are interested in setting policies and those who are concerned with monitoring basic standards of non-clinical care. It suggests that this division of interests and abilities usefully matches the two ongoing tasks of the Authority. The time that members give should be organised to take account of these different interests. In districts containing a Hospital Trust or Trusts the monitoring

of standards of non-clinical care will be a more important role for the non-executive members of the Hospital Trust(s) than for their counterpart in the DHA.

6. **Members should be helped to acquire the knowledge that they need to perform their role**. The development of teaching packages for financial and statistical information will be useful for any member who does not already have the necessary knowledge. There should be induction courses for new members who should be told, when they are appointed, that they are expected to attend. Periodic seminars on particular topics and a members' information room can be useful.

7. **The general manager should be accessible to non-executive members** and the chairman should not raise any objections.

8. **DGMs should show that they care, and care deeply, about providing a good service to the community**. Otherwise some non-executive members may see them as unfeeling administrators.

9. **Members should cultivate as wide a variety of local contacts as they can** with managers and other staff, region, local authorities, GPs, private hospitals, members in other districts and voluntary bodies. Doing so will improve their understanding of what is happening in their district that affects the health service and can provide managers with useful information.

10. **Chairmen need to be good at chairing DHA meetings**. It is a more difficult task than that of chairing many other bodies because they have a difficult role of acting as arbiter and broker between managers and non-executive members and often between different members if they pursue sectional interests. Chairmen need to recognise that they may benefit from training.

These are useful steps towards achieving the ideal, but it is the spirit in which they are undertaken by chairmen, executive and non-executive members that is most important. All need to want to make them work but to do so they must also be realistic about the constraints of time and knowledge that limit what non-executive members can do.

Two conclusions from a study of outside directors in British companies are relevant to the relationship between executive and non-executive members:

    '. . . there is a kind of dependency relationship between non-executive directors and executives. The non-executive director needs to keep the good opinion of his executive colleagues, since they are, after all, the people who will eventually implement [or not] the decisions which he is instrumental in reaching.'

The study suggests that friendship between the two can get in the way of judgement:

'The feeling seems to be that executives are bound to be partisans in terms of their relationship with the chief executive. If non-executive directors become too friendly with the executives, this partisan viewpoint may, in some way, rub off, and the non-executive director will lose the all-important quality of objectivity.'[11]

Leadership in the DHA has parallels with leadership in other relationships because the same general guidelines apply, as Peter shows in case study 4. These include, for the DGM, knowing what you want to achieve, exemplifying it in your actions, and making members, particularly non-executive members, feel important.

Many of the opportunities for taking a lead in the DHA necessarily take place at meetings hence the discussion of sharing leadership within a group, on pp. 69–70, is relevant for all those involved: chairman, members, and DGM.

SUMMARY

1. The Ideal

The major ideal in the new DHAs should be to develop shared values and trust between chairman, DGM and members. All those involved should seek to ensure that the DHA plays the following roles:

- responds to the community it serves,
- judges the relative priority of different interests within national policies,
- defines and monitors the standard of care,
- shows appreciation of good staff performance.

The DGM and other senior managers should accept that the DHA has a useful role to play and do their best to help non-executive members to contribute their individual abilities.

2. Difficulties in Achieving the Ideal

(a) The *dismissive attitude* that some DGMs and senior managers may still have towards the contribution of non-executive members.

(b) Constraints of *time* and *knowledge* limit non-executive members' ability to understand complex issues, or to know the services in their district, and, therefore limit the contribution that they can make.

(c) Problems that may arise in the new DHAs through members not being sufficiently sensitive to, and concerned about, local views.

3. Steps towards the Ideal

Experience with DHAs before the NHS review showed that they could be made more effective by improving mutual trust, clarifying the role that members play and the information that they need. In future it will be important to clarify what the new DHAs should be discussing, how they are going to monitor effectively, and how to make the best use of non-executive members. All members will have a potential leadership role to play at times, and the chairman and DGM an essential one. The non-executive members will need to take the lead in giving an outside perspective and in responding to views of the local community.

7 Leadership in the Region – District Relationship

'if an RGM is not seen to be leading on some things, then there is something terribly wrong with the relationship with DGMs'. (RGM)[1]

'You get the region that you deserve.' (DGM)

There are many different opportunities for leadership in the relationship between a region and its districts. The regional chairman, RGM and senior regional managers should have a vision of *where they think the region should be going*, and seek to lead the districts towards its realisation. Those in the districts should have their own vision for their district, which may not coincide with that of the region. Further they may – and should – have a view of where the region should be going. They can try to lead others towards their vision. So there may be *competing visions*. That is far better than having no views at all, because it means that people *care*, and have a positive view of what they think should be achieved.

THE IDEAL

The ideal, it should be remembered, is the *nature of the relationship* that leaders should be seeking to establish, and the *results* that they should be aiming at. It makes no judgement about the *nature of the organisation* and the *division of responsibilities* between region and districts.

Mutual Respect and Understanding

This is, of course, an ideal for all relationships, but it is mentioned specifically in this chapter because it can be particularly hard to achieve in relations between two different tiers in a large organisation. **Mutual understanding means understanding the role that each has to play, and the difficulties that that involves.** A sympathetic understanding is even better – that is, a capacity to *put yourself in the other person's place*, so that you know how the work of the Service looks from there and can appreciate and sympathise with the problems of playing that role. The understanding should be both *general* (of the work and problems of the other tier) and *specific* (of that of the individual with whom you are dealing).

Mutual respect requires a belief that values are shared, and that both tiers are doing their best for the Service. It also requires a belief that the *other tier is performing its role effectively and efficiently*, even if there are reservations about the nature of that role. Mutual respect, like understanding, has a general aspect in terms of the overall view of the other tier, and a specific one concerning the judgement of individuals.

Mutual Pride in the Region

The ideal is a mutual pride in the region, and a desire that the region should compare favourably with other regions. This means that managers in each tier not only want to do their own work well, but to *help others in the region to do so, too.*

A pride in one's region is desirable because it can help to make the relationship between region and district, and between districts in the region, more effective and encourage mutual support. Both regional and district managers may at times benefit from each other's help. This is more likely to be forthcoming if they share a common concern for the effectiveness of services in the region. People work better together if they share *common goals.*

It may be argued that regions are artificial creations made up of very different types of districts, and therefore providing no sensible basis for pride and common goals. The larger and more diverse the region, the stronger is this argument. Yet where there are common policies there is value in trying to develop a feeling of common ownership of, and pride in, them. Doing so is likely to lead to *better policies*, and to *facilitate their implementation.*

Most large organisations have *intermediate tiers*. Unless overall policies and procedures are more efficiently laid down nationally (as they are in retail chain stores, for example), there can be advantages in having regional differences to cater for differences in circumstances and to encourage innovation. If there is a case – as there is in the NHS – for such differences, then it is desirable to strive to develop and to implement *distinctively good policies*. The successful development of such policies ought to be a source of pride for regional and district managers, and their chairmen.

Common Ownership of Policies

The previous arguments all pointed to the advantages of a feeling of a 'common ownership' of policies. Given the degree of district autonomy, it is even more important than in most organisations for the lower tier to be consulted in policy formation. **Sharing in the development of policies is the best way to encourage a feeling of ownership, and hence of *acceptance*.**

This ideal means that regional staff genuinely want to know about district problems and views, and wish to consult them at an early stage about proposed policy changes. It also means that senior managers at district level are willing to respond and to contribute to the development of policies.

Leadership by the RGM

The RGMs should give a lead in their dealings with DGMs, despite the ambiguities and difficulties of the relationship. There will be times when a *collective lead* is necessary, and others when it will be desirable. The RGM can also usefully play a leadership role with some individual DGMs in assisting them to acquire a clearer sense of direction, and in providing them with support in times of difficulty. The RGM should be sufficiently in touch with the DGMs to know when such guidance is necessary. Similar arguments apply to other senior regional staff.

Leadership by Senior District Managers in the Region

Good leaders in the NHS should want to lead wherever they can make a contribution to the Service. You should not just be concerned with your own responsibilities, but also want to take a lead in developing policies, and resolving problems of the wider group to which you belong. This is as true for district managers in their relations with regional managers as it is for unit managers in discussions with district managers. **You can – and should – lead *upwards* as well as *downwards*: 'lead upwards' in the sense of contributing to the development of the vision for the larger group, and in the resolution of its problems.**

Region as District Champion

Each tier in an organisation – indeed, each boss – should be the *champion of those below*, and seek to protect them from interventions by higher authority that can make it harder for them to carry out their work. Hence regions should act as champions in explaining district needs to the centre, and take the lead in adapting national policies to regional circumstances, rather than just acting as a postbox.

Region as Rigorous Reviewer of Performance

The region's review of each district should be a rigorous examination of district policies and their implementation and of its comparative performance. In doing so, the region should show a full understanding of the issues involved. It should also agree what it will do to assist the district, and then *do what it promised*.

Minimum Bureaucracy

The ideal is to keep rules and paperwork to a minimum, to have periodic reviews of the volume of paperwork between region and districts and of the need for particular inquiries and returns.

DIFFICULTIES IN ACHIEVING THE IDEAL

'They seem to think that we have nothing better to do than fill in their forms'. 'They set quite unrealistic deadlines for giving them the information that they ask for'. 'They have no understanding of the problems that we have'. Such comments are often heard when managers in units or districts are talking about people at the region. Similar comments are heard in many other organisations. Relations between tiers in a large organisation are always potentially difficult. Difficulties are likely to be greatest between an *operating tier* where the work of the organisation is done, and a *planning and supervisory tier* because of the differences in tasks, and hence of *perspective*.

There is always a danger of managers in a lower tier viewing the actions and attitudes of those in the higher tier as being unduly constraining, and as showing a lack of understanding of conditions on the ground. There are two reasons for this. One is the different perspective that those in the higher tier necessarily have as to what is important. This is a good reason. The other is not: it is that it is all too easy to lose touch with operations and, if you do not consult those on the ground, to design foolish policies and procedures. **The difficulties that regional and district managers in the NHS often experience in their relations with each other must be understood as part of the common problems that exist between separate tiers in large organisations.**

The relations between regional and district managers in the NHS are more difficult than those in most other organisations because of their *greater ambiguity*. This ambiguity arises in part from the existence of separate DHAs by whom the district managers are employed. There is a potential role conflict for district chairmen and managers between the expectations of the regional chairman and regional managers and those of members of the DHA.

The ambiguity in the relations between regions and districts has become greater because of the changes in ministerial expectations of the role that regions should play. Regions are the instruments for passing on – whether interpreted or not – the policy requirements of central government and for monitoring their accomplishment. An increase in such requirements, as there has been since the Griffiths reorganisation, is part of the more *dirigiste* approach to the NHS of the Thatcher government since 1979, compared with its predecessors. This has made the district managers feel more constrained at a time when they are expected to take on greater responsibility. The growth in the power of the regions is often seen by districts as *running counter to the aims of general management*.

Another reason for difficulty in the relationship is that *regions are responsible for allocating resources to districts*. When resources are very short, this is bound to be an invidious role, even though a formula for resource allocation can help to depersonalise the decisions.

The leadership role for the regional managers, and for the regional chairman, in relation to districts is additionally a difficult one because many district managers and DHAs are protective of their autonomy, and resent any actions that they see as reducing it. Regional managers do not have an accepted leadership role in the districts, though specialist regional heads may be able to establish a professional leadership. The ambiguity of the relationship between the RGM and the DGMs makes it hard for the RGM to be accepted as having a role to play in leading the DGMs; as one RGM said:

> **'My leadership role is getting the DGMs to do what I think they ought to be doing, either nationally or regionally and that I do not have the power to direct them to do.'**

The gap between district and units is potentially easier to bridge than that between districts and regions because they work within the same Authority. It is also easier because they will usually be physically nearer to each other and the DGM will have fewer UGMs to relate to than an RGM has DGMs. For these different reasons there are more opportunities for informal contacts between district and unit managers than between regional and district managers. Such informal contacts can help to build *mutual understanding*.

STEPS TOWARDS THE IDEAL

The Templeton study of DGMs showed that at that time (which was from the spring of 1985 to the summer of 1987) the large majority of the DGMs studied were critical, sometimes very critical, of their region. The criticisms were even greater than those one would normally expect between regional and district levels in large organisations. By the time this book is being read the situation may have improved as both regional and district managers will have had longer to sort out organisational changes. However, difficulties are sure to remain, so it is worth reviewing what can be done to lessen them.

Managers are in the best position to work towards more effective relationships between regions and districts, so most of the suggestions are addressed to them. Chairmen and members, particularly the former, have a potentially important role in the attitude that they adopt to the other tier, and in the interest that they take in the nature of the relationship between managers at region and district. All involved in the district will want to put to region the best case for resources for the district, and sometimes to enlist public support as well, but it should be possible to do this without denigrating the region. **The region can do more than districts to move towards the ideal, since the criticisms of the relationship are mainly made by those in districts who are on the receiving end of regional actions.**

Seek to Develop Mutual Understanding

The best way to understand the problems and attitudes of those who work in a different tier of the organisation is to *work in that tier*. The next best is to realise that because of your different jobs you will have a different *perspective*. So you need to make a real effort to try and understand their problems and how they see them. For regional staff, this means getting out into the field, taking a real interest and listening. For district staff, it means taking trouble to explain your point of view, and why you hold it.

A common criticism that is made of the level above, and one that is often made of regions, is that the policies drawn up do not take account of the pressures upon the tier below and of how difficult it will be for districts to do what is asked. Ideally, regional staff should understand the real impact of what they are asking for, including the dangers of a diversion of effort from work that may well be more important for the Service. **A step towards the ideal is genuine consultation of district views, which may at times be best done on the telephone** – best in that it is faster, and less time consuming than the bureaucratic consultation process with which the Service is familiar.

1. **Managers at region and at district can usefully cultivate relationships with those in the other tier whose cooperation they need.** Such network building is an important way of trying to establish *good communications* between the two tiers.

2. **The manner that regional managers adopt in their contacts with district managers will also help to determine how the latter feel about the region.** There is a difficult balance to be achieved here: regional managers should be – and should be seen to be – helpful and understanding of district problems, but also searching and demanding in the review of district performance.

Try to Develop Common Goals

1. **People work better together if they share common goals, and if these goals embody shared values.** The value of agreeing a formal statement of values was discussed in Chapter 1, and an example given of the common values adopted in the West Midlands Region. Even more important is a general acceptance by regional staff of the need to involve district managers in establishing common goals. It is one aspect of the general guideline that *people own what they help to create*.

2. The danger in relations between different tiers in an organisation is always that the lower tier will try to outwit and circumvent the policies of the higher tier – often they may need to do so to get their job done! **Human ingenuity at ignoring or getting round regulations should never be forgotten. The answer to it is not tighter regulations but trying to get an agreement on what are sensible policies and regulations.**

Developing Mutual Respect

Mutual respect is built on trust and on judgements of individual effectiveness. Staff managers, whether at region or district, will be consulted and used if they are judged to be able and helpful. They, like those providing a service to other managers anywhere, have to be able to *convince others of the value of their advice*.

Knowledgeable and Rigorous Performance Reviews

The criticisms that many of the tracer DGMs made of regional reviews were that they failed in both of these respects. By the time this book is published greater experience of doing the reviews should have made them better. Good reviews require (1) *prior work together* on the subjects of the review, (2) an *understanding* of the issues and of the relevant figures, and (3) a searching examination of whether the objectives, that should have been agreed in the previous review, *have been met*.

Cut Back Bureaucracy

A common criticism is that regions are *too bureaucratic*. There is always a danger in large organisations of bureaucracy increasing: a growth in the volume of paperwork, longer delays in approving submissions, more committees and a desire for more detailed control. In an organisation like a region there is unlikely to be a permanent victory over the growth of bureaucracy, just as there is no permanent victory over weeds in a flower bed. The options are preventive measures that discourage the growth of bureaucracy, regular 'weeding' of excesses, or periodic blitzes. Most important is a recognition that *bureaucratic weeds will flourish unless controlled*.

Developing Managers

IPR necessarily gives the regional chairman and the RGM a role to play in the development of general managers that can be used to do that and also to build bridges between region and districts.

A Leading Role for Districts, too

Districts can – and should – contribute to improving the effectiveness of their relationship with the region. However, there is a balance to be achieved between being helpful to regional managers, a useful source of advice and comment, efficient and competent in the return of necessary papers and yet challenging (where that is necessary) about the way that region is performing its role.

DGMs and other senior district managers with leadership ability can use that ability to persuade others of the desirability of changes in regional policies. Those who are new in their job, or who are meeting many difficulties, cannot – and probably should not – spare the time to play a leadership role in the region. Those who feel that their own patch no longer needs the same amount of effort and drive from them could usefully turn their attention to what needs doing in the region.

Options to Consider

1. **Developing an agreed statement of values.**
2. **Activities that can help to develop a greater mutual understanding and sense of direction.** Away days, or couple of days, is one commonly used method of doing this. They can achieve the advantages aimed at, but they have dangers, too, of making people feel more disillusioned and disengaged and of providing an opportunity for *focusing and strengthening disagreements*. They are therefore difficult to manage successfully.
3. **District managers should consider whether they want – and *why* they want – to take a more active role in regional affairs**, and weigh the potential *benefits* and *costs* of doing so. The potential benefits are: (1) becoming better known at region, which may be useful in discussions of the district's problems; (2) influencing regional policies and the satisfaction of playing on a wider stage. The costs are mainly those of *time*, particularly having less time to spend within the district and on district affairs.

SUMMARY

1. The relationship between a region and its districts offers opportunities for leadership by all those involved in the relationship. There may be competing visions, but that is far better than having no views at all, because it means that people have a *positive view of what should be achieved*.
2. The *ideal* is:

– *mutual respect* and *sympathetic understanding* of each other's role

and the problems associated with it;
- *mutual pride* in the region;
- *common ownership* of regional policies;
- *leadership* by the RGM and *support* to DGMs in difficult times;
- the region acting as *district champion* in relations with the centre;
- the region making a *rigorous and knowledgeable review* of district performance;
- a *minimum of bureaucracy*.

3. The major *difficulties in achieving the ideal* are:

- common problems in *relations between two tiers* in a large organisation which have different roles to perform;
- the *ambiguities* in the region–district relationship;
- *changes in ministerial expectations* of the regional role, which increase the ambiguities.

4. *Steps towards the ideal* are:

- developing *mutual understanding and respect*;
- trying to develop *common goals*;
- improving *regional review of districts*;
- *cutting back bureaucracy*;
- districts *contributing to regional policies*.

5. Bureaucrats write: leaders mainly *talk* and *listen*, as that is the way to understand other people's views and problems. That is the way to test the value of your vision, and to persuade others of its value.

8 External Leadership

'Relationships [with MPs] are built up, not when you are in a storm, but rather patiently and over a long period of time, when neither side is in trouble.' (John Harvey-Jones)[1]

Many staff in the NHS have to work with people outside the NHS, other than patients. This requires two different forms of leadership. The first is to take the lead with NHS staff in setting and observing *appropriate attitudes to the local community*. The second is to *lead in these external relationships*. The latter can often be more difficult than leading subordinates, because you will have less power to influence what is done.

The more senior the post, the wider the range of people outside the NHS who should be influenced. The main organisations, groups, and individuals with whom DGMs should establish productive relationships are: CHC, social services and other parts of the local authority, FPCs and GPs, media, MPs, voluntary organisations, various community groups, environmental health services, trade unions and the private sector. UGMs and general managers of Hospital Trusts may have as wide, or nearly as wide, a range of external contacts, and many other staff will have to relate to some of them.

THE IDEAL

You must know what you think is the ideal to aim at in relations between NHS staff and the local community if you are to take the lead in shaping local NHS attitudes. The following are suggested as the ideals that should be pursued.

That *NHS staff* will:

1. Accept that there is a **responsibility to account to the local community** for the service provided.
2. Seek to **understand** public wishes, community health needs and inequalities in health, and **take them seriously**.
3. Care about the **district's reputation in the community** and seek to ensure that it has a good reputation for its services, and is known as a good place to work.

4. **Make the best use of resources in the community** that can
    achieving common goals.
5. Practice a **more open style of management**, so that those in-
    terested in the community are consulted and kept informed
    about policy changes.

**If you are to be successful in leading your external contacts, you
should pursue the following ideals in your relationships with them:**

1   **Recognise your interdependencies** and agree on common values
    and goals that you both want to pursue.
2. Seek to **prevent or overcome mutual suspicions** so that you trust
    each other to work towards these common goals.
3. Having agreed your common values and goals, **work supportively**
    to achieve them.
4. Where there are differences of values or of interests you will **deal
    honestly with them**.
5. Seek to **understand** and take account of, **the roles, interests and
    attitudes of the other(s)** and the constraints to which they are
    subject.
6. Encourage voluntary effort, and **treat voluntary bodies/helpers** as
    partners.

DIFFICULTIES IN ACHIEVING THE IDEALS

There are four kinds of difficulties here. First, the common difficulties that arise when people from *different organisations* have to work
together. Second, difficulties that arise from having to work with
diverse groups who may have *different interests*. Third, the difficulties
that arise from *your own attitudes* and those of other NHS staff to the
role of the community or to particular groups. Fourth, *specific
difficulties* that arise with particular organisations or groups.

Common Difficulties in Relations between Organisations

1. The natural tendency for people to *identify with their own group*,
    and to be suspicious of outsiders.
2. *Mutual ignorance* of each other's work.
3. *External pressures* upon one or both organisations.

Relations with Diverse Groups

You may have to deal with *many publics*, some of whose interests *conflict*.

Your Own Attitudes, and Those of Other NHS Staff

There is always the tendency for professionals to think that they know best and that public views are uninformed and mistaken. This may be true, but it should not be the starting assumption.

In your own attitudes, you may exemplify the common difficulty described above, of regarding those who do not work for the NHS as alien outsiders.

You may disregard the value of voluntary effort; as Long and Harrison say:

> 'In a highly professional organisation, which any health service in the western world must be, voluntary effort is usually seen as peripheral, at best symbiotic and at worst parasitic in its relationship to the health care system. It will need a considerable indoctrinal effort to modify these attitudes at all levels within the medical and nursing professions.'[2]

Now with the health service under considerable pressure there is a different danger in some districts: that *more* help will be expected from voluntary organisations *than they can deliver*.

Difficulties with Particular Organisations

Each of the different groups poses its own distinctive difficulties in achieving the ideal. Those familiar with the relationship may be all too well aware of these difficulties, but they are worth mentioning for those who may later need to work with such organisations.

1. *The CHC* is poorly funded, and has been called a 'watchdog without teeth'. Therefore, you should not overrate what it is possible for CHCs to do in researching community and patient views. Further, they cannot provide an overview of what the public wants; as Long and Harrison say:

> 'If the collective experience of CHCs since their inception in 1974 is examined it becomes clear that there is no such thing as

a general public or whole population that is actively aware of, and concerned about, the wide range of health service issues that exists at any one time (Hallas, 1976). There are many publics with specific interests.'[3]

These are the difficulties for the CHC in speaking for patients: shortage of funds and difficulties in identifying public wishes. Then there can be difficulties in the relationship between NHS managers and the CHC secretary, chairman and members. These can arise because the latter feel that they are largely ignored by NHS managers and not given adequate information or warning of district policies. From the NHS side, the problems may be seen as the CHC opposing changes (particularly closures) that managers believe to be necessary, or of the CHC not doing their job properly, talking about minor problems rather than paying enough attention to patient welfare. On both sides there will be differences in attitudes: some managers will not accept that the CHC has a useful role to play; some will, but may be critical of how well they do it; and some CHCs may be inherently suspicious of managerial attitudes. The competence of CHC secretaries and of members will also vary, as will that of the NHS staff.

2. The *local authority* can be difficult to deal with because officers have to respond to the politicians in power. There will also be problems of the distribution of costs on any joint project. A further problem in some districts is that *more than one* local authority may be involved. (The problems of developing effective relations with social services are not discussed here because such comments may date if there are changes in community care.)

3. The main difficulties of working with *GPs* is that they are independent operators, who value their independence. They have a major influence upon the health Authority by the way in which, and the extent to which, they make use of it for their patients. They also affect the demands upon its resources by the attention that they pay to health promotion.

4. *Press* relations can be a minefield for the inexperienced. The difficulties of working with the press will depend upon the character of the local papers. A particular difficulty is that the press are often more interested in what is *bad news* from the point of view of the health Authority, rather than in favourable news. Another is that misquotation, quotation out of context and

factual errors are quite common. Press reports can stir up local opinion, particularly against closures of small hospitals.

5. *MPs* of a different party from that in power can cause difficulties because they may want to make political capital out of problems faced by the local health services, MPs of any party may cause difficulties by supporting opposition to the DHA's plans.

6. *Voluntary bodies* pose problems because of their diversity and the fluctuating nature of voluntary help, although this will vary with the level of organisational ability. Some of them may be pressure groups whose particular concerns may conflict with the needs of other groups and with the judgements of professionals and managers in the district. Problems can also arise from a voluntary body raising money for a particular purpose, such as buying a CAT scanner or building a hospice, and then leaving the district to pay the ongoing costs.

7. *Community groups* can cause problems because of the intensity with which they may support a particular cause. As an American book puts it:

> 'Sometimes community groups can behave like perfectly civil adults. They schedule appointments, make their case on the merits, listen to your side and accept a reasonable compromise. But not often. More common is the ritual ... confrontation, abuse and impossible demands.'[4]

Even if 'more common' is not so true in the UK, there are parallels.

8. Relations with *trade unions* are usually amicable, but occasionally an issue arises that causes considerable concern amongst affected staff, leading to protest action in places. National grievances will be wholly or partially outside local control – partially because good local relations may help to minimise industrial action. Some hospitals have a history of poor industrial relations that makes life more difficult for a new manager.

9. Problems with the *private sector* are likely to arise from their selective case mix, acute work rather than long term chronic work, creaming off potential income for the NHS from private patients and from their diversion of consultants' time. There may be particular difficulties from the feeling amongst some NHS staff that any relationship with the private sector is a betrayal of NHS principles.

STEPS TOWARDS THE IDEAL

Clarify Your Own Values

You cannot hope to achieve the ideal of agreeing common values and goals with your external contacts unless you have both *clarified* your own values, and these are values that you can expect people in external organisations to be *willing to share*.

Your attitude to consumerism is a major example of your values. It is also an indication of how far you are responding to the wider social changes discussed in a report by the Organisation for Economic Co-operation and Development, which said that 'increasing administrative responsiveness is an essential challenge for advanced industrial democracies'.[5] Consumerism for the public service has been described as caring and citizenship,[6] and citizenship as meaning active participation by the individual.

It is possible, as David King has pointed out:

> 'to be in favour of consumerism without believing that consumers are always right and professionals invariably wrong, simply that they have some obligation to debate and reason with each other'.[7]

Believing in consumerism also means believing in the right of choice and of information. Neither used to receive much attention in the NHS, but there are encouraging signs of a change, such as principle 8 in the philosophy of care for nursing, midwifery and health visiting (on p. 48), which starts:

> 'Nursing has an obligation to offer choice to patients/clients and to uphold their right of self determination.'

and then goes on to explain what this means.

How you view the existence of the CHC, or any successor to it, is one guide to whether you really believe in consumerism – that is, that in a public service the public has a right to a say in the nature of that service. You should ask yourself how often in practice, whatever you say that you believe, you think that professionals know best, and that there is no useful role for consumer bodies in a particular decision.

Your attitude to community groups is a parallel guide to your values. Such groups can be very useful, as two American writers (one of them formerly Administrator of the New York City's Health

Services Administration) point out:

> 'they know, see and suspect things that even the best manager may miss. They provide a mirror . . .
>
> While community group tactics may be unpleasant, offensive, or just plain unnerving, it is critical for the public manager to remain objective about the merits of the complaints. Have they got a point? Why do they feel this way? What can I do about it? These are the questions that should be on the manager's mind in any community group encounter . . .
>
> Community groups represent your customers, and they are often right, or at least partly right, in their complaints. If you cannot accept this proposition, you ought to be in another business.'[8]

Your behaviour towards the press is another indication of your values, and whether you really believe in the public's right to know. How you react to criticisms in the press that have some justification is another guide to your values. One DGM, who recognises and accepts the role of the press, commented ruefully after an unfavourable news report on the care of young long-stay patients: 'the story made me a bit angry and a bit vulnerable, so it was quite good journalism'.

Your attitude to voluntary organisations is yet another indication of your values. The tendency is to treat them as supplementary appendages who are to be told of decisions rather than as partners to be consulted in advance.

Understand public concerns, and practise public accountability.

The history of CHCs can provide general guidance about public concerns. Long and Harrison point out that they have three recurrent concerns:

> 'strong loyalties for smallish local hospitals which can offer human-scale services; accessibility of services, including transportation problems in rural areas; and the level of services provided for the elderly, the mentally ill, and mothers and children'.[9]

These are a useful guide to the kind of criticisms that your CHC may make of new proposals, and hence to the kind of discussions that you should be having with them. If your proposed changes are contrary to these values of proximity, human-scale services and giving priority to the care groups named, then you are likely to meet opposition. You will need to explain especially carefully why you think they are necessary, and to review what could be done to meet their concerns.

Your attitude to the DHA, if you are a senior manager, is one guide to your approach to public accountability, so are the other actions that are taken to consult, involve and inform the DHA and the public. The main steps that have been taken in districts with a strong concern for public accountability and for consulting the public are:

1. *Improved public information.* E.g., using the media, producing a readable annual report and easy and attractive guides to using district services and entering hospital, and providing information about the treatment and management of different illnesses. The latter supplements what doctors communicate, since they do not have the time to go into sufficient detail and the patient may not be in a state to take in the information when told of the nature of his or her illness. An interesting example of trying to meet the latter need is the telephone information service with 200 tapes jointly developed by The College of Health, Gloucester and Exeter Health Authorities.

2. *Surveys of patient opinions of the service provided*, pioneered more than thirty years ago by the psychologist Winifred Raphael. They are becoming more common again, though they are valuable only if they lead to *action* to remedy criticisms.

3. *Involving the public in the planning of services and making the services more accessible.* North Manchester, the winner of the *Sunday Times* 1988 competition to find the top NHS team[10] cited the diverse work that it was doing to improve consumer contact and to provide a more accessible service. This included evolving a consumer participation working group to examine the best ways of using feedback from users of the services, involving them in the planning and development of services and developing an advocacy service to help patients with problems.

David King maintains that:

> 'the single most important step to be taken in making the NHS more user-friendly would be the general adoption of something like locality planning, dividing up districts into localities based on natural communities each with its own participative arrangements to involve consumer representatives in planning and service delivery'.[11]

He points out that this will require *staff training* to change old attitudes.

Make Good Use of External Resources

To do so can require a radical change of attitude, perhaps by yourself as well as by your staff. It means thinking more broadly about what resources are available, or potentially available: asking yourself, or researching, what special interest associations can be used to increase or enhance the facilities and service provided. It means accepting that people other than professionals can help the sick and can promote better health. It means thinking both about what organisations exist in the community that could be helpful, and considering how to encourage their birth and development. The creation of self-help groups of various kinds is one example, as an American writer has pointed out, though the comments apply in the UK too:

> 'Increasingly, previous consumers of service are becoming providers of service. Their effectiveness is generally quite good. For example, groups formed and maintained by alcoholics, abusive parents, widows and cardiac patients, among others, have been able to support and sustain their members in ways which the professional community could not.'[12]

Build Relationships

John Harvey-Jones's advice in the quotation at the head of this chapter, of **building good relationships as a protection against later trouble**, is an example of a general guideline that is relevant to many kinds of external relationships, and especially to MPs and trade unions. There are also more specific steps that apply to relations with particular organisations.

The first step to building good relations with the *CHC*, and trying to ensure that they can contribute to the effectiveness of the services provided, **is to show that you take them seriously**. This is true, too, of other relationships, but it applies particularly to the CHC as they may feel at a disadvantage compared to the district because their resources are so limited and they are dependent upon the district for information. They can easily resent the way that they are treated and, like most other people, will respond to being *consulted*. The DGM attending some at least of their meetings is one way of showing that they are taken seriously. Informal monthly meetings between the DMT and the CHC to explore items on their respective agendas was a method that worked well in one of the tracer study districts.

One DGM who aimed to attend as many meetings of the CHC as he could (about two-thirds), taking the appropriate managers with him, explained why:

'I am there to take whatever flack is thrown, to be available to help discussions, to educate the CHC members to be more objective and less political in their criticisms, and to maintain good relations with the chairman and secretary. I can clarify issues and promise action where that is possible. That tends to defuse a lot of problems and it is also important to show that someone senior is taking a positive interest in their activities.'

The information that is provided for the CHC needs to be *clear* and *easily assimilated*, since the CHC is composed of people from different backgrounds, knowledge and levels of understanding.

It can help to establish guidelines for the relationship between the CHC and the DHA, as the North West Thames Region did after a survey of CHCs in the region showed very variable relationships with districts. The guidelines, endorsed by the RHA in 1985, recommended eight good practices.[13]

The media, and especially newspapers, need *news*. A recognition of that is the first step to building a good relationship with local journalists. If you make it easy for them to get news by providing press releases and press conferences when there is something newsworthy, good or bad, you can help to establish good relations. The aim should be to establish such good relations that the news editor will phone to check any allegations against the district.

The Templeton tracer study DGMs were very aware of the need to build good relationships with the local authority(ies). They sought to do this by meetings with the chief executive of the local authority and the director of social services, often together with the DHA chairman. They also made contacts with education, planning and housing. This is the 'precautionary' relationship building referred to in the quotation at the head of this chapter. The building of relationships at the senior level can help to keep everyone in touch with intentions. Chairmen who have a political background can often be very helpful here, because they will have more experience of working in a political context.

There needs to be relationship building at the operational level, too. Decentralisation of some care decisions to local groups composed of social services and NHS has been found a good way of helping to ensure that they work together. One example is setting up a patients' care committee with members from the CHC, voluntary organisations, social services and health service professionals.

Relations with FPCs are important because of the influence that the FPCs can have on GPs who are gatekeepers to much of the NHS. Establishing and maintaining contact is a way of keeping informed about their plans, and by early discussions seeking to influence their thinking. The proposals for large GP practices in *Working for Patients* will make them a very important contact for managers of hospitals.

Voluntary organisations are a potential resource that you may be able to use more effectively. You need to show them, and your staff, that they are taken seriously. If you consult them in advance of decisions about changes – for example, Mind about changes in services for the mentally ill – you give them the opportunity to present the patients' viewpoint on these changes. You also enable them to say whether your expectations of what they can do are realistic. Further, it gives them warning of the likely *repercussions on their own services* – for example, more people coming to their day centre because of a closure of an NHS service. Accept invitations to speak to voluntary groups. Attend their annual general meeting to put across your current objectives.

More general relations with the community can be cultivated in a number of ways. A common one is an open day. This has the additional advantage that it can be used as an opportunity to involve more junior members of staff and help them to display leadership skills – good for talent spotting, too. Encouraging the League of Friends by showing an interest in their activities is a way of trying to develop the commitment of those who have already shown an interest.

General Guidelines to Leadership in External Relationships

Leading NHS Staff
1. **Set a good example to your own staff, and to others in the NHS, by showing that you care about what the public thinks and that you are trying to provide a user-friendly service.**
2. Set a good example, too, by the way that you **talk about people in other organisations**. Do not talk disparagingly about them. Show that you take them seriously, and seek to understand their views and problems.

3. **Be aware of your staff's attitudes to their external contacts.**
    Realise that some staff may be genuinely concerned to do their
    best for the patient, but believe that they will know what is best
    and that consultation is therefore unnecessary. They may be
    dismissive of the contribution that lay people and staff in other
    organisations can make. If you think that your staff's attitudes
    are contrary to your ideals for external relationships, seek to
    change them. You may be able to provide *training* that will help
    to modify their attitudes. An away day to talk through the
    problems of dealing with a particular external group can also help
    to bring out underlying attitudes, and to explore the reasons for
    them.

Leading in Your External Relationships

1. Be alert to *what is happening outside* – that is, scan the
    environment where you work for possible threats to what you are
    trying to accomplish, or opportunities to further it. **Such alertness
    is crucial in a general management job.**
2. **Be proactive: take preventive action to try and forestall any
    threats and seek to capitalise on any opportunities.** For example,
    consider in advance the likely reactions to a neighbourhood
    home for a small group of mentally handicapped people, and
    who might be able to help in getting a more sympathetic attitude.
3. **Develop good sources of information about the attitudes and
    intentions of those who can affect the work of your department,**
    unit or district – for example, know who are the people who
    really matter when you want to get support from social services.
    This means either building your own network or using that of
    others in the district – some chairmen can be very helpful here.
4. **Seek to get agreement on what are the shared values that underly
    your working together, and then on the objectives to pursue**; only
    then move on to the specifics of who is going to do what by when.
5. **Learn to adapt to the different culture of the organisations with
    which you are dealing.** Be aware of the pressures that may divert
    those in other organisations from doing what has been agreed,
    such as political pressures affecting social services. Try to fore-
    stall these if you can, and build contingencies; for example, to
    protect you against the local authority not cooperating in housing
    for the mentally handicapped or sheltered accommodation for
    the old, develop contacts with local housing associations.
6. **Recognise that in many of your external relations you are in**

practice *negotiating*. **Good negotiation requires understanding what the other person wants** – that is, what *really matters* to them, the *constraints* within which they are working and what *you can offer them*.

Whether you apply these general guidelines in practice will depend upon your values, how proactive you are, how good is your network of relationships and how skilled you are at understanding other people's attitudes and situation. It will also depend upon whether you are able to lift yourself above the pressure of day-to-day work and problems to notice what is happening in the *wider environment*. You can improve your leadership ability by learning to be better in each of these respects, hence the inclusion of Chapter 12 on Developing Yourself.

Reviewing Your Relationships

In jobs where you have to deal with many groups in the community, you can find it helpful to list all the individuals and groups who can *affect the achievement of your objectives*. This is a check on whether you are ignoring, or paying too little attention to, those who could matter to you and to those who work for you. Next, consider the *present state* of each relationship, if indeed one exists, and where you should try to establish, or to improve, that relationship. Such an analysis is illustrated in Figure 8.1 for a DGM, though a similar approach can be used by people in other jobs.

Draw a diagram like that one illustrated in Figure 8.1 and insert your main external contacts. You can put both individuals and groups. Then rate each one from +3 to −3 for each of the following:

1. The *importance of their support* for achieving your objectives.
2. *How far they are supporting them*; examples of ratings here are:

    +3=Already support them or are easy to lead in the directions that I want.
    −3=Actively pursuing objectives in conflict with mine.

3. The amount of effort that I am giving to *building/improving* this relationship.

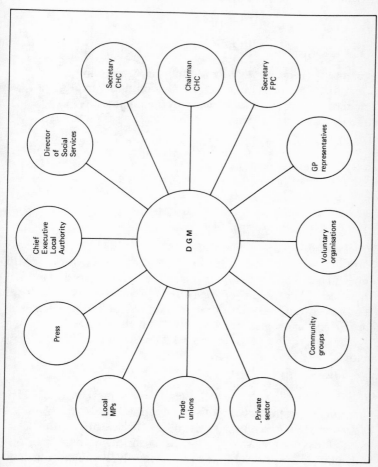

Figure 8.1 Network analysis of external relationships: illustrated for a DGM

SUMMARY

Leading in your external relations requires two different kinds of leadership. One is to lead *NHS staff* so that they have the right approach to their external contacts and to the local community. The other is to lead *in the external relationships themselves*.

1. *The ideal*

(a) That *NHS staff* will:

–   recognise their *accountability* to the local community;
–   seek to *understand* public wishes and community health needs;
–   care about the district's *reputation* in the community;
–   make the best use of *resources of help* in the community.

(b) That *you will* in your relationships with external contacts:

–   agree on *common values and goals*;
–   seek to prevent or overcome *mutual suspicion*;
–   *work supportively*;
–   seek to *understand* their roles, interests and attitudes;
–   make good use of *external help*.

2. *Difficulties in achieving the ideal*
    There are two common difficulties that come from working with people in another organisation: suspicion of outsiders and mutual ignorance. There are problems that arise from having to deal with many publics whose interests may conflict. There is a temptation for professionals to think that they know best. Then there are particular problems in relations with individual organisations.

3. *Steps towards the ideal*

(a) *Clarify your values*. Your attitudes to consumerism, the CHC, the press and voluntary organisations will all show your values.
(b) *Understand public concerns* which, as the history of the CHC shows, focus on the values of local facilities, human-scale services, and giving priority to the old, mentally ill and mothers and children.
(c) *Improve public accountability and consultation* in the planning of services.
(d) *Make good use of external resources*, which may require a radical change of attitude in yourself and your staff.

(e) *Build good relationships* as a protection against later trouble.
(f) Set a good example to your staff, and to others in the NHS, by showing that you *care what the public thinks*. Be aware of your staff's attitudes, and if necessary seek to *change* them.
(g) Be *proactive* in your external relations.
(h) Learn to understand and to adapt to the *different culture* of other organisations.
(i) Review your external relationships in terms of their *importance for achieving your goals*, and of how *satisfactory they are*.

Part III

Leadership in Action

This part of the book illustrates how individual managers in the NHS, from different backgrounds and in a wide variety of jobs, *think about* and *practise* leadership. It provides practical examples of many of the points made in earlier chapters. Part III is also intended as a contrast to the other parts of the book. Some readers are likely to prefer it, some may like the combination of analytical chapters and personal examples; some may find Part III too anecdotal. The intention is to cater for these individual differences, since we learn in different ways. My hope is that most readers will welcome the combination because it provides two complementary ways of examining their leadership role.

The first chapter in Part III (Chapter 9) compares fifteen young leaders' views on leadership; to what they attribute their career progress; how they see their future; and what advice they would offer to others. Its aim is to encourage young managers, in all the activities that make up the NHS, to:

1. *think of themselves* as leaders;
2. *review their own views and actions* by comparing them with the other young leaders described in the chapter;
3. consider what they should do to *improve their leadership ability*, and to prepare for their desired career.

A further aim is to stimulate their elders to give more attention to *developing subordinates* who have leadership potential.

Chapter 10 is a case study of one of the DGMs in the Templeton tracer study. It describes his view of leadership, and how he seeks to lead, thus illustrating points made in earlier chapters. It also describes how his principal contacts view the role he plays.

Questions are suggested at the end of the general discussion and after Case Studies 1–3 and Case Study 4, so that readers can more readily use each account to consider whether they contain lessons for their own leadership style.

9 Fifteen Young Leaders

This chapter provides examples of what fifteen young leaders across the range of most of the occupations in the Health Service had to say in answer to questions about their views on, and approach to, leadership. The fifteen were found by asking a variety of people for suggestions of young leaders in different kinds of job. 'Young' was set at under 35 for all except medical UGMs and the DGM who were considered young if they were under 40.

Each was asked the questions given in Appendix B (p. 188), either face-to-face or by phone. They were sent the questions in advance, and most had prepared their answers before the interview, which included supplementary questions as appropriate. They were sent the interview notes for checking. All but two were happy for their name and position to be given. The interviews took place in the summer of 1988, and the ages given are at the time of the interview.

The chapter is in two parts: first a summary and illustration of answers to the questions that elicited the most useful replies from twelve of the young leaders, and second three individual case studies which are an abbreviated transcript of the interview. The latter are marked by * in the list below. The three are leaders in general management posts at different levels and from different career backgrounds. Their answers to the question about leadership actions that they had observed are included in the first part of the chapter.

DETAILS OF THE YOUNG LEADERS

The fifteen listed, from the youngest to the oldest are:

Janine Smith, Senior Employee Relations Officer, North West Thames Regional Health Authority. (Age 28)
Sue Baker, Clinical Practice Development Nurse, Wandsworth Health Authority. (Age 29)
Lynne Clift-Peace, District Dietician, Community Unit, South Derbyshire Health Authority. (Age 29)
*Heather-Jane Sears, Hospital Manager, Didcot Hospital, Oxford-shire Health Authority. (Age 29)

Breda Avil, District Chiropodist, North Bedfordshire Health Authority. (Age 31)

Catherine Jones, District Physiotherapist, North Bedfordshire Health Authority. (Age 31)

Philip Burton, Associate General Manager, Patient Services, South West Hertfordshire Health Authority. (Age 32)

Dr Iain Robbe, Director of Public Health and Planning at Worthing District Health Authority from September 1988. (Age 32)

Heather White, Senior Assistant District Treasurer, Kettering Health Authority. (Age 33)

Jo Yates, District Occupational Therapist, North Derbyshire Health Authority. (Age 33)

Sue Machell, Neighbourhood Nurse Manager, Wandsworth Health Authority. (Age 34)

Chris Ellarby, Principal Assistant Treasurer, Basingstoke and North Hampshire Health Authority. (Age 35)

*Mike Marchment, UGM Community and Mental Handicap, South East Staffordshire Health Authority. (Age 37)

Dr Roland Starrs (pseudonym), UGM acute, London non-teaching health authority. (Age 37)

*Alan Burke (pseudonym), DGM. (Age 39)

This group obviously does not include many other leaders at more junior levels, most notably ward sisters, though two of the group have been ward sisters earlier in their career.

ANSWERS TO THE QUESTIONS

What is leadership?

It can be hard to describe leadership, though as one DGM said, 'you know it when you see it'. All the young leaders were able to answer the question, though some were more certain of their answers than others. The most common description involved giving direction and having the tenacity to ensure its achievement, but all gave more elaborate descriptions, and some emphasised other aspects of leadership, for example:

'Leadership is part of the management role, especially in times of trouble and crisis; then you need to encourage individual loyalty so that people have someone to follow. Leadership means being the figurehead, a role model and the representative of the department'—Catherine Jones, District Physiotherapist.

'It is the ability to persuade whoever one is working with to identify with common aims and objectives'—Dr Iain Robbe, Director of Public Health and Planning.

'It involves motivating staff in a clearly specified direction; encouraging, monitoring and generally being a positive influence'—Lynne Clift-Peace, District Dietician.

'Acting as an agent for change'—Philip Burton, Associate General Manager, Patient Services.

How to lead

Self-confidence was seen as very important – 'if you have not got this, how can others be confident in you?' – as was *consistency in behaviour* and having a *sense of humour*. Several talked about the need to adopt a different approach for different people and situations, sometimes being assertive and sometimes seeking to influence. Several, particularly but not only the women, stressed *participative leadership* and the importance of *motivating people*:

'By following the example of the people who influenced me most: by encouraging participation and giving others lots of responsibility'—Breda Avil, District Chiropodist.

'By giving people as much responsibility as possible, but backing them up and not leaving them to flounder. That is the way I have been treated and the way that I want to work with my staff. It is not so much a boss/subordinate relationship as working together'—Janine Smith, Senior Employee Relations Officer.

A few used the word 'inspire' to describe what they were trying to do:

'I try to inspire the professions, particularly those where I have no direct influence. It is mainly having self confidence . . . I want freedom for people to make mistakes, the freedom to achieve'—Dr Roland Starrs (pseudonym) UGM acute.

'I try to lead by inspiring others, by communicating with each individual, understanding what they want out of life'—Lynne Clift-Peace, District Dietician.

'inspiring people to be innovative'—Sue Machell, Neighbourhood Nurse Manager.

Some stressed the need to *explain the significance* of what had to be done:

'I try to motivate people by explaining how important it is and what happens if it fails and their roles in it so that they can see the end result'—Chris Ellarby, Principal Assistant Treasurer.

A different kind of answer to the question: 'How do you lead?' was:

'Only infrequently is it up front leadership, usually it is more discreet and subtle than that'—Dr Iain Robbe, Director of Public Health and Planning.

'acting as a catalyst and taking a more backseat role in influencing people, e.g. "can we try and do this?" ... "let's see how this works"'—Sue Baker, Clinical Practice Development Nurse.

Many other points were made, including the importance of not doing anything to *threaten the trust* that is being built up.

Leadership opportunities in my job

The fifteen described some common opportunities for leadership in their jobs, often that of motivating and encouraging staff, but their jobs also differed in their opportunities for leadership:

1. The greatest opportunities, but also the most difficult, are offered by the general management jobs: 'greatest' in terms of the range of people who can be influenced and of the possibilities to shift the direction of the group for which they are responsible, whether a hospital, a unit, or a district; 'most difficult' because of the complexity and the variety of often conflicting interests.
2. The district paramedic jobs offered the opportunity to be the leaders of their profession in the district.

The jobs in the first and second groups are up front leadership ones. The third group are different:

3. Those in staff roles can lead those whom they advise by seeking to influence their decisions. At the most senior levels, which are not represented amongst this group of young leaders, they may also have a sizeable staff to lead.

The answers of three of the general managers to the question: 'what are the opportunities for leadership in your job?' are illustrated in Case Studies 1–3, the fourth said:

'One of the key opportunities is to put out the message that people have freedom to make a mistake and can go away and manage . . . people learn from their mistakes. I have to manage when there are more mistakes than achievements'—Dr Roland Starrs, (pseudonym) UGM acute.

The paramedics spoke of the need to *lead*, and to *speak up for*, their profession:

'Leading the profession in the directions that it needs to go. Representing the profession to the unit and district general managers'—Jo Yates, District Occupational Therapist.

'On the clinical side it means setting standards and ensuring that we live up to them. Having quite strong views about the development of the service so that one can argue the case for resources'—Breda Avil, District Chiropodist.

Speaking up for their profession could also include making a professional contribution in multi-disciplinary groups:

'Few dieticians have taken a strong managerial line. The profession has always been very ladylike, genteel. If you are that, no-one will notice. By example I can show that you can be successful, a woman and a caring professional'—Lynne Clift-Peace, District Dietician.

The physiotherapist spoke of the need to influence clinical behaviour from a managerial perspective:

'Most physiotherapists are working in ways that they would not choose to do, so that one's role is to help to make the difficult management decisions more palatable . . . I have to lead in terms of the clinical compromises that have to be made'—Catherine Jones, District Physiotherapist.

Those in staff jobs at the second or third level necessarily gave other kinds of examples of opportunities for leadership in their jobs:

'Speaking up first in meetings of the unit management board tends to influence the way that people think before they have made up their minds . . . If you go in first and then follow that up by saying what we could do about it, then you can influence people'—Chris Ellarby, Principal Assistant Treasurer.

'One of the issues is implementing quality of assurance initiatives within the acute services unit. This involves negotiating and marketing one's ideas with a wide range of professions'—Philip Burton, Associate General Manager, Patient Services.

Sue Baker, the Clinical Practice Development Nurse, described one of her leadership roles as questioning doctors about the products they are using in their care plans. Her questions were backed by research.

'Initially doctors felt threatened but now they consult me about what I would like them to do. This has helped other nurses' confidence. The younger nurses use research and their reading to challenge practice'.

She was the only one to pick out a particular care group as offering many opportunities for leadership. She said that this was true for care of the elderly because there is a lot going on and many ways where care can be improved.

Do you think of yourself as a leader?

Most did very strongly, but a few had reservations or had not done so before being asked the question. Those who gave very definite answers said:

'Yes, because I am in a leadership role, and because I have quite clear ideas of where my service should go, but I am flexible enough to change if there is a better way. In the past leadership was not seen as a positive attribute, particularly for a woman'—Breda Avil, District Chiropodist.

'Yes, not only within financial management but also in other groups by taking the forefront when required in discussions, for example, on planning issues. Also bringing together other people's ideas into a precise statement'—Heather White, Senior Assistant District Treasurer.

'Yes because the DMO is the only doctor in a position to give independent advice and to bring a sense of balance to a discussion of the different issues involved'—Dr Iain Robbe, Director of Public Health and Planning.

Some of the less definite answers were:

'Only when I get asked the question. I have not really thought about it. I lead because no-one else is leading'—Dr Roland Starrs, (pseudonym) UGM acute.

'Not naturally, but if I think about it there are a number of things that I do that are leadership. I also endeavour to influence leaders ... Now I see myself as supporting general managers'—Chris Ellarby, Principal Assistant Treasurer.

'Some of the time: I think that I am learning to be a leader. I think that my head OTs see me as a leader when I am pioneering in areas of weakness'—Jo Yates, District Occupational Therapist.

Examples of leadership actions

Few gave examples of leadership actions that they had seen. One said: 'I see examples of good chairmanship but not of leadership'. It is hard to be sure of the explanation for this poor response: is it a discouraging reflection on the extent of leadership in the Service, at least before general management? Is it that managers in the Service may not be attuned to thinking about leadership, even if it is there? Or that people do not distinguish between management and leadership? Or that some were only thinking of their own leadership?

The general managers found it easier to give examples, probably because their experience was wider. Overall very few examples were given. Those that were can be divided into three groups: (1) risk-taking, (2) innovation together with the capacity to sell new ideas, and (3) people management, which were examples mainly given by the women.

1. *Risk-taking*

> 'our director of finance who decided that the regional package for information technology was not suitable. He took the district out of it at considerable expense and risk and by perseverance managed to win through. That was inspiring'— Mike Marchment, UGM Community and Mental Handicap.

> 'When I was very young, seeing an administrator take on a bunch of consultants who wanted an answer. Giving them the answer "no" without denigrating anybody and in a way that left no room for repercussions'—Alan Burke (pseudonym) DGM.

2. *Innovation*

'Ken Jarrold, when President of the IHSM created a very clear vision of what the Institute should be doing, with a tremendous projection of ideas, so that he gave the Institute shape and direction. He started initiatives like a radical reappraisal of its educational content'—Alan Burke (pseudonym) DGM.

'We are moving in a non-NHS way in personnel in this region by aiming to provide a core group of skills, but the rest to be available if people pay for them'—Janine Smith, Senior Employee Relations Manager.

3. *People Management*

'when I was a staff nurse at University College, Sister Manger, MBE, was tremendous, quite old school, but you really knew where you stood. She was always very, very fair and she was always the same no matter what'—Heather-Jane Sears, Hospital Manager.

'My present boss is very good at motivating staff. She never expects one to do something that she cannot do herself and will talk it through with you if you have problems'—Jo Yates, District Occupational Therapist.

'The district treasurer in Coventry was an example of leadership by giving people responsibility, encouraging them according to their potential, and in that way getting the best out of the staff'—Heather White, Senior Assistant District Treasurer.

Do you see yourself as a role model?

Only some knew the phrase 'role model', which means an exemplar, someone to model one's behaviour on in the job. Even if most of the fifteen gave few or no examples of leadership by others, did they see themselves as exemplars? The women seemed to be more conscious of the importance of being a role model – see the chapter on Leadership and Nurses for a long discussion of this by Heather-Jane Sears. The other two nurses also stressed their responsibility to be a role model.

One likely explanation for the women's greater emphasis on being a role model is that it is still relatively rare for women to be seen as leaders in the Service, so that those who are feel a greater need to be a role model; for example:

'Yes. I try to come across as with-it and sensitive and as up-front professionally as possible'—Jo Yates, District Occupational Therapist.

'I see myself as a role model, for example in meetings, in conflict situations and in personnel situations as in the past a dietician would automatically have backed down in discussions even if she was in the right. Also in interdisciplinary meetings a dietician would not have made an input, now we do do that'—Lynne Clift-Peace, District Dietician.

It was not solely the women who saw themselves as role models:

'Yes, both in public health and planning. On the DMO side, as an example of an independent approach to problems and on the planning side, of how it is possible to balance a concern for getting the administrative work right, with also doing the strategic thinking'—Dr Iain Robbe, Director of Public Health and Planning.

Do women lead differently?

There have been several references to the women giving somewhat different answers to the men: attaching more importance to being encouraged and to encouraging others; citing more examples of good people management as examples of good leadership, and being more conscious of acting as role models. Does that suggest that women lead differently? Most, when asked the question, said that in their limited experience they thought that women did. The main differences suggested were:

'Women lead more gently. They can often get away with more because they do not go out for confrontation: they don't go for the kill but are trying to achieve rather than to annihilate opposition.'

'Women may take the credit more for the department than for themselves.'

'Women are somewhat more perceptive of the unspoken cues at meetings. They lead more participatively. They want to be part of the group and yet still lead it.'

'They are better at people-management, more sensitive and better at influencing others.'

Readers may like to know that an American survey of research and theory in 1981 concluded that:

'the preponderance of available evidence is that no consistently clear pattern of differences can be discerned in the supervisory style of female as compared to male leaders, although individual studies have been able on occasion to find some positive indicators, but not necessarily in the same directions.'[1]

What do you feel you have learned as a leader?

A common area of learning was skills in *understanding and dealing with other people*:

judgement: weighing up the opposition amongst colleagues very quickly and assessing the capabilities of one's own staff; knowing whom you can rely on and whom you cannot.

how much I still have to learn; how encouraging my younger senior staff can help me to get the job done; the problems posed by delegation and giving people freedom.

a much greater understanding of people and human nature – e.g., 'if you treat people with respect, they do the same to you'.

tolerance of individuals; learnt from my mistakes; learnt the ability to handle situations; to adapt my style according to the individual: some need coercing, some need to be told, some will get on on their own.

'you have got to make the most of what you have got and the situation which includes the people around you'.

'the importance of not beating around the bush but meeting issues head-on'.

Others learnt more *about themselves*:

'how pig-ignorant I am about management and that there is a whole science out there'—Medical UGM.

'the difference between my own view of myself and that of others. I thought that I was perhaps too democratic, whereas others see me as somewhat autocratic. This was quite a shock, indeed almost a relief as I had worried that I was too soft, but it does mean that I shall have to watch how I put things.'

Several of the women spoke about *confidence*:

'I have gradually learnt to feel more confident, helped by lots of positive feedback.'

'You need to learn the art of acting, of appearing confident even if inside you you are scared . . . most importantly is learning to be confident.'

'I have worn a uniform since I was four. I feel I was more prepared to come forward when I was in uniform as I was visibly representing my profession. Here we do not wear them: my boss said: "are you sheltering behind a uniform?" I am having to learn to dress as a manager.'

All spoke of what they *still needed to learn*. As one said:

'there will always be a lot to learn. The worst danger would be if in five years' time one thought that one had mastered it, because there are always likely to be radical changes.'

Many spoke of the *personal qualities* that they still needed to learn, such as patience, being more assertive, recognising that one's expectations may be too high.

Outside leadership activities?

All were asked whether they had outside activities which involved leadership. Nearly all said 'no', some saying that much of their time was with their family: Lynne Clift-Peace who has been married for five years, and worked throughout, has two step-children now 7 and 9. Sue Baker with two young children said that all she had time for was acting as a parent representative at her children's nursery group. The few others that said 'yes' were asked to describe their outside activities and to say whether they had contributed to their understanding of leadership. Sue Machell thought that her active involvement in the Health Visitors' Association had been helpful. The more detailed replies, other than from the young leaders described in the case studies, were:

'They do tend to see me as a leader at college [for her Diploma in Management Studies]. If people do that then you start to believe it yourself. Sometimes, though it can be quite exhausting. After a long day I occasionally sit back and say "I am going to let someone else take the initiative and do the organizing"'—Catherine Jones.

'On the work-related side I am branch secretary of the Oxford branch of the Health-care Financial Management Association. My recreational leadership activity is being in charge of stage make-up for the Northampton Gilbert and Sullivan Group. This involves bringing a team of amateurs together and trying to make the best use of their wide-ranging abilities. This is a manual skill unlike my work. I think it has helped my leadership abilities because of the need to lead a wider variety of people'—Heather White.

'As captain of the cricket team, I have learnt the importance of motivating and coordinating players to play above their ability. From my potholing experiences I have learnt that another leadership quality is the ability to know when to keep quiet; if somebody wants to take charge it is important, sometimes, to keep quiet and let them otherwise you can waste time arguing about who is going to take the lead on the descent'—Philip Burton.

Advice to someone aspiring to do your job?

This question produced a lively response from all fifteen. Their replies should provide useful guidelines for those wanting promotion, particularly for the more ambitious. There was advice about what you *should be*, and what you *should do*:

'recognise your weaknesses and take actions to remedy them whether they are personal or professional'.

'be flexible, be prepared to take things on'.

'be different, do not follow the trend'.

'you need to be bright, energetic, have good health, be a good communicator, know what to do and how to get there'.

'work hard: one needs to put the job first as you progress upwards'.

'you have got to know what you want to achieve and what you can give to the organisation'.

'don't wait for it to come to you . . . knock on doors get to know the people who can help you, it helps to smile and make it known if you are interested in a particular job. I have got my previous two jobs because of the contacts that I made.'

Several of the younger women stressed the need to have the confidence, even the cheek, to apply for jobs when you are the youngest applicant.

Sue Machell, the Neighbourhood Nurse Manager, also gave a different kind of advice: the need to believe in the *philosophy* of the organisation and in the philosophy of neighbourhood health care, as well as in the rights of the client. She also stressed the importance of keeping clinically up to date and of having a clinical aspect to the job.

There was advice, too, on managing your career. The managers in Case Studies 1–3 all talk about this. So did some of the others, for example:

'have as broad a base of experience as early as you can, even of dull things like sitting on committees; get yourself into as many situations as possible; tackle things that may daunt you a little because in that way you learn'.

'be aware that in my job you may be seen as a hatchet man'—UGM acute.

'get qualified as soon as possible, since qualified accountants are scarce in the NHS'.

'look at every aspect of the speciality, don't get focused too early in community medicine: so take your time and see what is available'.

Catherine Jones, the District Physiotherapist, spoke of the need to get over the conflict between the clinical and the managerial view-points. She thought that being a superintendent was a very useful role transition, and that you should stay at that level until you had made the transition. It means a change in priorities and values, for example:

'Before I argued about the importance of treating patients as individuals. Now I find myself arguing about the need to treat patients in groups ... Now I see things from the managerial viewpoint as that is my responsibility. I have to think in terms of efficiency. I have to balance loyalty to the Authority and to the profession.'

What and who helped you to get where you are?

Many of the answers were similar to the advice to others described above. Some thought that it was primarily their *own determination and personality*, together with getting professional qualification(s). Some also said that it was being in the right place at the right time: having to act up because their boss was sick or died. Some also, particularly some of the women, said how much they had been encouraged and supported by their boss(es) and others, including their husband or boyfriend.

The two doctors gave distinctive answers. The acute UGM with a medical background thought it was the situation that he found himself in:

> 'When I joined the district as the first specialist of my kind I was faced with obvious things that needed putting right . . . I was, therefore, involved in major change without management training. I was thrown in at the deep end and I swam . . . It was the situation that needed changing which helped me most in entering a managerial career and adopting a leadership role. Since I have been a UGM the flak and the responsibility have helped me to get where I am.'

Dr Iain Robbe, the Director of Public Health and Planning said:

> 'Principally the DMO in East Berkshire, who suggested that I read books and articles about management systems and change agents and who I observed taking a leadership role. This was the stimulus to becoming interested in the DMO work rather than in academic community medicine.'

LOOKING FORWARD

Some of the fifteen had only recently been promoted and were not yet thinking about their next move. The decision for those who were not general managers was whether to seek progression in their own speciality or to look to general management. One, Heather White, the accountant, was going to be seconded for three months in her district to help one of the UGMs who was not well. This would also give her the opportunity of deciding whether she preferred to go for a treasurer's post or a UGM's. Philip Burton spoke of what he would need to learn to make the transition to a UGM post:

> 'you have to cope with a great deal more responsibility, you have to learn to be more flexible and to be better at negotiating, marketing and selling ideas'.

Some had already more or less reached the top of their professional ladder at an early age so their next move could be as assistant UGM. Lynne Clift-Peace, the District Dietician, expected to stay five years, and then hoped to make that move, meanwhile taking a distance learning MBA which is more suited to a woman with children. She said:

> 'It is easier since Griffiths for young people to get promoted, but there still tends to be too narrow a view both in terms of the age that is suitable for promotion and of professional background.'

The manager in Case Study 3 at the end of this chapter describes how he planned his career to get into general management from an untypical background.

MAKING USE OF THESE EXAMPLES

Answer the same questions, which you will find in Appendix B. Doing so will make you reflect on whether – and if so, how – you lead.

For the under 40s[1]

1. Compare your answers with those given above. Note what is *different*.
2. What are the main *lessons* that you could draw?
3. Raise some of the questions in informal discussions with your colleagues as another way of learning more about how other people seek to lead and to manage their careers.

For 40s+

1. Who are the *potential leaders* amongst your staff?
2. In answering that question, how widely are you *talent spotting*?
3. Review what you are doing to *encourage* and to *challenge* them. What more could you do?
4. Are you an *active coach*? You should be helping your staff to lead more actively and more effectively.
5. What will your staff learn about leadership from *your behaviour*? What more could you do to be a good role model?

Case Study 1

Heather-Jane Sears, Hospital Manager, Didcot Hospital

Heather-Jane is young for the job she holds. She was a national finalist for the Young Career Woman of the Year. She was selected as a case study because she is unusually articulate about how and why she leads as she does, how she manages change and how she manages her career. She gives plenty of examples of what she does that illustrate many of the points made in Chapter 2 on Leading Subordinates. You will have met references to her in earlier chapters particularly to her views on the importance of being a role model for her staff in Chapter 3 on Leadership and Nurses.

Heather-Jane was 29 when interviewed in July 1988. After taking her A levels she travelled around the world for a year to enable her to think what she wanted to do. Meeting different people from different backgrounds made her realise that she wanted to work in nursing. She trained at University College Hospital, London qualifying as a staff nurse in 1982. A year later she became an acting night sister and took her qualifications in intensive care nursing at Guy's. Then she spent six months in South Africa travelling around and working in field hospitals. Her first sister's post was in 1985. Within a year she became acting nursing officer covering Guy's at nights. She came to her present job, where she has 80 staff, in 1986.

LEADERSHIP

What is different about your present job from the previous one?

It was a great contrast from a high tech acute London teaching hospital to a small hospital where I am general manager. Previously I had not done much care of the elderly and I had no district nursing training.

What do you see leadership as being?

A dynamic process whereby the leader influences others in order to achieve a common objective. I see it as someone taking the initiative, giving others direction, caring and sharing, not dominating.

It is the ability to enlist cooperation of people who initially are not keen to get involved, for example, the energetic staff nurse organising a Christmas review.

What are leadership skills?

Two way communication: the ability to talk and to be understood and to listen.

To give encouragement: some people need it and must be made to feel that their contribution, however humble, is still wanted.

Understanding staff's individual needs, like the sister who really knows her staff well, who knows who can cope with what. Everybody is very different and you cannot treat them all the same. It is interesting in general management because one has such very different groups of staff. There are the domestic staff with whom I communicate quite differently than with the physiotherapists and the doctors. They all have something to offer and they are all equally important.

Do you think of yourself as a leader?

I have always thought of myself as a leader. I was always the ringleader at school, team captain, head girl, and the editor and in nursing that went on. I think there are natural leaders: if you have a crisis there will be somebody who will come forward and take command. You do not have to be an extrovert to be a leader; you can develop into leadership.

How do you try to lead?

I am a democratic leader, but not laissez-faire. It is very important to get feedback from staff. You cannot really change things unless you take staff with you.

Integrity, fairness and consistency – consistency in mood and discipline – all are important. It is often these characteristics rather than position in the hierarchy that will command respect from those being led. I think you can really be quite firm and disciplinarian provided you are seen to be fair and reasonable, to listen to the other person's point of view.

I am quite a black and white person. I speak my mind. I have high standards and expect them of myself and of others, but people are individuals, some can do better than the base line.

I see myself as a change agent. I think I have skill as a facilitator. I will drip-feed ideas. I can implant ideas and get people to think that they are their own. I will pick off key members before staff meetings to implement change. I use my personality to sell ideas – people say that I ought to be in marketing rather than the health service! One reference said that I excel in the art of verbal persuasion. I was not quite sure how to take that. My father always used to say that I could sell sand to the Arabs.

Persuasion is part of being a nurse because it is an art that you learn. You have sometimes to persuade patients to do things that they do not want to do. Similarly you have to persuade and cajole staff into doing things rather than tell them.

A sense of humour is absolutely essential and I look upon work as fun. You have to keep a sense of humour, especially in the health service where it is very important to have a high morale. All my staff will work so hard and they are so dedicated as long as the atmosphere is good and morale is high, that means giving opportunities, delegating, educating, being cheerful, caring for them, treating them as individuals.

People need reassurance and constant praise. They work extremely hard and everyone is ready to criticise – I remember that throughout my training as a staff nurse. They need praise to keep going, everyone does. – Those fresh flowers are from my staff. I feel appreciated and I appreciate them.

You have to take some very tough decisions. You have to stand by your staff's mistakes as well as your own. It is really important that you stand by people when the going is not good: that gives you credibility. It is that that they will remember when you leave.

What are the main opportunities for leadership in your job?

Encouraging staff, particularly in times of stress, for example, a primary nurse who is nursing a terminally ill patient that she is doing a good job, or a nurse who is doing a first teaching session in front of others.

The buck stops here: accepting responsibility is part of my job. If all else fails and we cannot get staff then I have to take decisions like shutting casualty. If staff are at an unsafe level then I have to come in and do it.

Being available for support: making sure that people know that I do not mind being phoned at home (behind her desk is a large sign giving her home telephone number). It is never abused, but staff do ring me quite a bit if only for reassurance that they have done the right thing, particularly a junior staff nurse if sister is not there.

Being a champion; I have to deal with the press, do a lot of public speaking promoting the hospital or explaining why we are shutting beds. If Radio Oxford turns up at the doorstep everyone thrusts the microphone into my face.

Do you see yourself as a role model?

Her answers to this are given in Chapter 3 on Leadership and Nursing, pp. 39–40. She also said:

'As a figurehead I have to be assertive, it might be to the consultants with a complaint from a relative. It is often in front of staff so I have to be a role model. I think learning to be assertive in primary nursing is quite important.'

Do you see your activities outside work as being leadership ones?

I have always been the social organiser for activities. I had done lots of fund-raising and that is very useful here. I joined the Business and Professional Women's group which involves public speaking. I was a national finalist for the Young Career Woman of the Year and so I got invited to lots of clubs to speak. I am on the branch executive of the Royal College of Nursing and also on the General Management Special Interest Group at national level. The Royal College has a national view of what is going on and that helps my work here immensely; it also gives me contacts for information.

Learning to speak was very useful, though I hated it at the start. It is very important for a leader, particularly in a community like this where you are the figurehead, that you can speak properly. If you are trying to get people to fundraise for you, particularly for the elderly who are not glamorous, you really have to sell it. It is important to be a good, moving speaker to do that.

I am very much involved in the community here. I run a carers' support group. I also get involved with groups that help the hospital. I have started an activity programme for our patients so that it should not be such a very long dull day. I have local groups and schools and churches involved so that we have all sorts of things going on here now: everything from animals coming in to aerobic classes and pantomimes. That takes a lot of community involvement and it is very important in PR terms.

This is a small town, though it is growing fast. It is a community and the person they look to is the matron of the hospital. I am still seen as the matron. I am the figurehead here; anybody who wants to know anything about health will get in touch with me or write to me. It is the same as being the head of the police and the mayor – there are really about five key people in Didcot.

What have you learnt as a leader?

A lot, above all I have learnt to appreciate my staff. I have learnt financial management, communication, time management and confidence, having to be the figurehead has given me confidence. People have looked to me as a leader so I have had to do things even if I am quaking inside. I always think I look calm outside: 'serene as a swan on the outside, yet underneath I am paddling like hell'.

I am naturally quite assertive, but I have had to learn to be even more assertive. It is knowing how to say 'no' firmly, and to give reasons why.

I have had to learn to delegate. Nursing is probably a bad kick-off point for this because nurses do not like to be seen as lazy. To move from nursing into management you have to get completely away from wanting to jump around. I always remind myself that I cannot do everything. Delegating not only gets the job done it also develops staff.

I think that I have changed as a person. I like to think that I am a better person now. If you have learnt to care for people more and to have a better understanding of them, that makes you a better person. Perhaps a little harder in some respects, I do not know if that is good or bad, but you have to take some very tough decisions.

What do you still need to learn?

A lot, you can always learn to communicate better, to be better at time management. I need to improve my writing skills. The higher up I get in management, the more I need to write better. I need to learn about strategy and long term planning: in my next job I shall look for one that will give me more of an overview. It is very easy to get tunnel vision when you are stuck in the woods.

What/who helped you to get where you are?

Two people: one my tutor on a staff nurse development programme at Guy's and the other a nursing officer, a man, who was a tremendous manager and from whom I learnt a lot as a night sister. Both of them told me that I had ability and potential. They made me think: 'gosh, if they believe in me and they see a lot of people, then I must believe in myself'. That gave me the confidence to apply for jobs. It is very important to believe in yourself.

All along I have applied for jobs for which I did not have the qualifications requested; for example, the sister's post I applied for said three year's experience and I only had one; I applied for this job after only one year as a sister. I had to put up with people saying: 'don't be ridiculous, of course you cannot be a hospital manager, you do not have the right experience'.

I am a very independent person. I left home when I was fifteen due to family problems and I have had to work quite hard. I have always taken a pride in my work, so I think that I have pushed myself along.

Career planning rather than job searching has got me where I am. I have not drifted into things as it is so easy to do in nursing: each job that I have taken has been for a reason. Nurses so often move sideways and stumble through their careers. You do not have time to do that nowadays as it is very, very competitive. If you are going to get there, then you really must plan.

I chose to be a night sister because of the broad experience that it gives you, I worked in every single area of the hospital. On night duty you are a much closer team. Because of the vast area you cover as a night sister, you learn to organise your priorities. One reason why I took the course in intensive care is that it is one of the most demanding; if you have done that you can do anything.

My area of expertise in entering management is not just nursing, it is very much personality, being able to deal with people. I have also had a lot of teaching experience. I have always been interested in teaching, counselling and dealing with staff.

My interest in people has helped. I have travelled a lot and met different people. If you have an understanding of people from different walks of life, that helps in your job.

I always try to turn negatives into positives: instead of saying: 'nobody thanks me' turn it into a positive to remind yourself to thank your staff.

Advice to others?

Career planning: study your CV and recognise what is missing. If you keep your CV as broad-based as possible that will give you choice, because you do change and develop. But you must link jobs sensibly, so that there is a sort of direction which is not too narrow. You should plan to move just after the minimum time for that job. You should not leave too early as you must consolidate on your knowledge, but it is very easy to stay in a job too long. A year as a sister is the minimum because otherwise you leave the place in a worse state. I could have stayed as a sister very much longer, I enjoyed it, but if you are going to get on it is important to keep moving and to get different experience.

I am now considering whether I should move. I am quite happy here and could stay on much longer, but I feel that in any job you give of your best in the first couple of years when you have new ideas and you push and have a lot of energy. If you have a change then you push forward again. It is very easy to sit back after a couple of years.

You must look at your training needs after you realise what is missing in your CV. I did that. When I wanted a general management post like this one, I realised that I would have to manage the budget for the first time and that I did not have any financial experience. I was prepared to study and work at the same time and that means giving up things, also self-financing a lot in the health service. I took an Open University course in financial management. In my interview for here I stressed that this was a weak area and that I wanted and expected to have some training. I am taking the Diploma in Management Studies on day release, but of course I have to make up the time.

You do have to career plan, life is very, very short – it is not just a dress rehearsal. So you have to make the most of every day. It is absolutely essential that you seize opportunities when they arise.

OTHER POINTS

How I manage change

I had to change a lot here as it had not changed for a long time. I have gone on two speeds. There are some things that I thought were unacceptable: those I changed. A new broom sweeps clean; when you are new in a job is your best opportunity to make changes and I think people often miss it. The first stage in the job is absolutely crucial: you have got to find where is your kick-off point. People will accept change from the new manager provided you are not too radical. I wrote down a list of what I wanted to change and starred the things that I thought I could get away with changing straight away, which was quite a small area. Most of the change has been in attitudes and has had to take place over a long time and I have had to take staff with me. Implementing change is picking off key people, convincing them and working it through.

Knowing what the jobs are like

As a leader you must be willing to accept that you cannot know everything and must manage through people, but as far as possible you should try and do the jobs yourself. I am general dog's-body as well as being manager here! If we don't have a porter I will be emptying the bags. If we are short on the wards, I will be helping there. If we are short in the kitchen, I will be doing suppers. Which is good, because you actually are in the situation and you realise that you have been piling all that work on and you forgot the basics, like how long it takes the dishwasher to empty.

You cannot do everybody's job, but it does help if you have actually done it, even for one shift. You can understand what it is like from their side. It helps being a nurse; I understand the strains and pressures of being a nurse and so I can communicate much better than if I was an administrative general manager. I am very much a people person, I do not manage from an ivory tower, from an office.

Management methods

I use an action plan approach every two months. Eighteen months ago I instituted a system of individualised primary nursing care. We developed the plan for it together, and evaluate it every two months deciding what we could push forward and what is not working and should be thrown out.

I find it is good to have meetings with different groups of staff as well as more general staff meetings, for example, a meeting of nursing auxiliaries will say things they would not in an open staff meeting. I can then diplomatically feed these points back to the trained staff. It is better to have meetings when they are needed rather than as a regular thing. In informal contacts, having coffee with your staff, you learn more than you ever will in staff meetings.

I introduced performance appraisal for everyone from the top down. Untrained staff, such as domestic and catering had not been appraised before. You have to educate them that it is really a personal development interview to look at training needs, not a slap wrists session. I am now working on a reversed appraisal system from the bottom up. Eventually the staff will appraise me, which will be an excellent way to learn on the job and as a way of encouraging others to be open to constructive criticism.

Balancing work demands

Sport: I have to keep myself physically fit in a very demanding job. It can be very stressful, especially as I am by myself, top of the little pyramid here. Once during the last two years I failed to keep the balance between work and relaxation. I realised in time that I was getting too stressed, concentrating too much on the hospital.

I am asked to serve on working parties and all sorts of things. I enjoy that but they all take me away from here. You have to learn to say 'no'; otherwise you are out too much, and then one is not supportive. I think the main point of my job is being supportive. If I am on site whoever has a problem can come and find me. I am already away one day a week at my management training. Then I try to pop in first thing in the morning and at night. I am always here at 7 a.m. so as to have an hour with the night staff.

Price of leadership

It is really quite lonely. It may have sounded rosy – all my staff love me and give me fresh flowers – but it is not like that. If you have high standards, are trying to implement change to pull standards up and to stick within a budget you are not popular.

In my job I am professionally completely torn in two. Professionally I am on the side of the patient. I agree with the nurses and the doctors how terrible the cuts are. I will fight tooth and nail against them. But my job as a general manager is to live within the resources. You have to live with this tension. The doctors need to keep management in line, saying: 'what are we doing for the patient?' and the managers have to keep doctors in line by saying: 'we live in the real world'. It is a healthy tension, but a very stressful one for the general manager.

Professionally, I am used to making tough decisions: as a night sister deciding whether to resuscitate. You have to harden up. You have to be quite self-sufficient. You have to have confidence in yourself that you are doing your best. Everything is blamed on management, the whole morale and all the frustrations. The staff have to blame somebody: they cannot blame the patients, they cannot blame their colleagues, so they have to blame management. So you have to have very broad shoulders.

And its rewards

It is a wonderful job, too, you do get praise. People do say 'thanks'. It is the appreciation, the little comments that keep you going. Somebody gets promotion and writes you a letter saying what they have learnt by being here.

I enjoy the job, I work for twelve hours a day so you have got to enjoy it.

USING THE CASE STUDY

Answering the following questions can help you to do so:

1. What are the most distinctive aspects of Heather-Jane's account?
2. Do you see her as very much a leader? If yes, why? If no, why not?
3. Would you like to work for her? Why? or Why not?
4. What do you think is the most important thing that she says?
5. What do you think her staff will remember about her when she leaves?
6. What do you think about her acting as a general dog's-body?
7. Can you learn anything from her views on career management?
8. What are the main lessons for you from this case? Are you going to practise any of her advice?

Case Study 2

District General Manager

One interesting feature of this case study is that Alan Burke (a pseudonym) is a second generation DGM, who was able to start in the job with a clearer view of what he wanted to accomplish than could many of the first generation DGMs, who had to discover what the job was like as well as coping with the initial problems of reorganisation. Alan has a very clear view of leadership as being the creation of 'corporate style and direction' and of the need to put this across in many different ways and by one's own personal example.

Alan Burke, a pseudonym, is in his late 30s. He started in the health service as a member of the national training scheme. He has been in his present job for a year. Before that he was a UGM acute in the same unit where he had been unit administrator. His previous jobs included two in planning in other districts.

LEADERSHIP

What is different about your present job from the previous one?

My present job differs most from the previous one in its scope, much more time is spent dealing with boundaries and people outside the organisation. I am now more concerned with process rather than doing – this is more satisfying as it can be quite creative provided you know what should be done on the executive side.

I find this job less stressful than being an acute UGM. The pressures are less immediate and the diversions fewer.

What do you see leadership as being?

It is about values and clarity of purpose and continually reinforcing the values and purpose whether by performance reviews, by workshops or by going round giving out the right values. Everything one does and says must express a commitment to the values and purpose in one way or another.

Setting standards and the expectations of people's performance, continually stretching and striving.

Do you think of yourself as a leader?

Yes, I began to do so when I was a unit administrator because I thought of myself as running the whole unit rather than just my part of the organisation because I had a clear idea of what needed doing in a unit where not much had happened. It was apparent within 6 months that I was regarded as the leader by others including the consultants.

How do you try to lead?

Driving and inspirational rather than by influencing, I chose this approach deliberately when I came here, although I rather enjoy it. When I am talking about the need to be positive and not to denigrate the service and get growls of appreciation, then I know that I am in business.

However, one needs to be quite careful about the culture of the organisation and tailor how you work to that. I deliberately set out to be very dominant here, but I think that in the future I must become less so. When I have all the right people in place I must change and give them more space.

Create a vision of the future and to be able to describe it to others. That is a very difficult and nebulous art. I use workshops for managers which are on basic topics. During these I get people to consider our underlying values and they can become quite heavy idea sessions. I will use the same ideas in a different form with the aim of helping people to see whether they can use them.

Continually appraising the world and acting as a translator and synthesiser.

Continually reappraising our progress. It is possible to measure some processes and outcomes provided one is very clear about what you are trying to do. IPR, for example, is very easy if you do not do it properly but really establishing stringent objectives is much more difficult and we are learning to get them reasonably straight.

Some people find it very easy to drift off course, so one needs a strength of purpose. One has to demonstrate not only how to do something but that it can be done. For example we are going to set up a screening programme: those who are involved in doing it met obstacles and came back to me. Perhaps as a test of whether I could carry it through by confronting the opposition.

There are various ways in which you achieve street credibility. I picked the right issue for doing so when I was unit administrator and then I was home and dry. But it was also known that I was committed to making improvements and that doing so was important to me. Since for many of the medical staff in particular our institution represents their lifetime's work they will have confidence only in people who manifest this commitment.

What are the main opportunities for leadership in your job?

I gave some examples already. Leadership is needed in handling turmoil, for example a difficult closure requires considerable leadership. It is needed for clarifying the purpose of the organisation and establishing understanding of that within the workforce. One needs it, too, when one is pushing through major organisational changes. Also when one is dealing with very difficult personal matters such as people, whether managers or clinicians, who are not capable of performing optimally where they are. One's authority for dealing with that differs between those two groups, but the persistence with which it is dealt with should be the same.

Ultimately, though, leadership is concerned with creating corporate direction and style.

Do you think of yourself as a role model?

What is that? Yes, in that I am showing people that I want them to work in this way and think of their work like that: a high standard of performance and hard work. I am deliberately and cynically enthusiastic and energetic every day whether I feel like that or not and that is a hell of a strain on the family, who see the private person with their guard dropped.

Provided one has the vision right other people may be the role model, there needs to be a choice of models.

Leadership activities outside work?

None, I deliberately steer away from that now – IHSM activities are not outside work.

What do you feel you have learned as a leader?

People actually do want direction, to know which road they are on and whether the pace that they are going at is right, but people need freedom within that framework of purpose and direction and they do not want their action unduly constrained. Most people can do things well beyond their assumed capabilities, although in the NHS we do not encourage that.

Still need to learn?

How to avoid executive work. I am spending too much time on that and not enough on the externalities and direction, although I am fairly ruthless about what I do.

Still think along tramlines. I don't think laterally enough. I am not doing anything about development yet, I gave myself a year on this job first.

Is the price of leadership worth it?

Unequivocally yes, I like doing it, I like the power although I realise the limitations and dangers of it. I like being at the top of a large organisation. I try to manage balancing this with my family commitments in a reasonable way. It requires careful organisation and my wife is immensely tolerant. I limit my outside activities but I would rather be doing the job than a lot of outside activities.

What/who helped you to get where you are?

Being an acute UGM, as it is difficult for people who have not had an acute post to get a DGM job from inside; being quite active in the IHSM as one gets known.

Advice to someone aspiring to be a DGM?

Something that I did not do: have a very clear-cut career development plan to ensure that you have experience of a range of functions and move in and out of staff and line jobs. Be ready to move every two to three years.

You have to work for somebody good at the job. I learned a lot from the DA in my previous district. He retrieved my career as I had not been sufficiently centrally involved and I needed to find my way back into unit administration. I had not been keeping sufficiently on top of extra-curricular work like IHSM, nor had I worked for good people before. Getting experience of planning was helpful but that happened by chance rather than by design as it should have.

Building your network; this is important both to get on and when you are there.

Be ruthless with yourself, and make that demonstrable, in never allowing things to be fudged – unless by conscious decision – to ensure that difficulties are handled.

OTHER COMMENTS

There is a new orthodoxy about leadership and there are dangers in that; as an organisation we must remain tolerant.

The reality of change below the top in the NHS is very small, and so is the commitment to change among large sections of the work-force and indeed in significant numbers of senior managers one meets.

USING THE CASE STUDY

1. What are the most distinctive aspects of Alan's account?
2. What do you think is the most important thing that he says?
3. What are the main lessons for you from this case? Are you going to apply anything that he says?

Case Study 3

Mike Marchment, UGM, Community and Mental Health, South East Staffordshire

This case study is of particular interest because of its advice on how to make the transition to general management from a specialised background; the particular attention paid to management development as part of a drive to improve quality and as a way of encouraging corporate cohesion; and Mike's analysis of the changes that he should seek to make in his personal characteristics in order to become a better leader.

Mike Marchment is 37. He qualified as a dentist in 1975. From 1975 to 1978 he was in general dental practice. From 1978 to 1980 he was in Papua New Guinea, the first year as a provincial dental officer and in the second year as a service planner for a World Bank project. From 1980 to 1981 he was at the University of Birmingham taking his Masters in Community Dental Health. From 1981 to 1984 he was a salaried general dental practitioner part-time and part-time clinical dental officer in salaried service. From 1984 to 1986 he was a district dental officer in his present district. He has had his present post for two years and eight months.

LEADERSHIP

What is different about your present job from the previous one?

Three things: the breadth of the area in which I was involved, the variability from day-to-day and the status which was conferred by the position, so that I was perceived as having knowledge about mental handicap and community health services despite having no experience of them.

What do you see leadership as being?

Setting direction and ensuring its achievement.

Do you think of yourself as a leader?

Yes, if you look through my CV you will see that I have never been a deputy, I would find it difficult to be someone else's deputy.

How do you try to lead?

I try to lead by influence, by inspiration and by direction. These are not mutually exclusive and they are in that order, though I think that sometimes one has to short circuit influence and inspiration and go to direction.

What are the main opportunities for leadership in your job?

I have been leading in four areas:

1. In information technology.
2. Introducing locality management.
3. Formulating the mental handicap strategy in agreement with the social services.
4. Developing a management development programme which over the last three years has taken 10–15% of managers' time. This programme is unique and I have written it up in the *Health Services Review*. In the first year the 20 managers worked together in small groups, looking at problem-solving with the necessary academic background to do so. In the second year they were operationalising this, developing service standards which are included in service manuals for each care group. These activities serve the purpose both of supporting a drive for quality and of encouraging corporate cohesion. This year we are developing management skills more, using the service manuals as the benchmark for what is happening in their own departments.

Do you see yourself as a role model?

Yes, but only as a role model in my own discipline, not as a UGM because I think my background is too atypical. It is a safe bet for people to model the more common administrative background.

I see myself as a role model in the dental discipline and have been a slight irritant by challenging our practices, arguing that we must be accountable and prove that what we are doing is correct.

Do you have leadership activities outside work?

No, but within work related activities, there are the following:

– I like to take jobs where I can get my ideas incorporated in education;

- I am chairman of the local British Dental Association;
- I am the Programme Secretary of the IHSM;
- I set up and I chair the community UGMs' group in the region;
- I am on the board of the Financial Information Project, which is a national involvement and helps us here to ensure that we are developing in the right way.

What do you feel you have learned?

One needs respect to do one's job, not love. One almost does not have time for that. The loneliness of power is true, I miss the fact that I cannot afford to become friendly at work, that is quite tough.

There are no secrets of management, merely commonsense and most important of all, nous and it is very difficult to teach that.

What do you still need to learn?

Maturity, because I cannot trade forever on being the young, bright thing. I need to learn humility. It is painful to discover that people do not like success: there is nothing that public servants like less. I need to remember that.

I need to learn to be more assertive and less aggressive. I can confuse direction with aggression. So it is not management theories that I need to learn, but these personal characteristics.

What/who helped you to get where you are?

My ambition. I have been and am ambitious to get on and make 5-year career plans.

The post-graduate management training that was part of my Masters.

My strong university links: honorary senior lecturer in one department, and honorary research fellow in another.

Building up relationships with authority members in my authority.

Building management relationships with key people in the district.

Working on a regional group which gave me contacts with DGMs and UGMs so that I became known as being interested outside dentistry. The group was on health promotion and enabled me to bring back money into the district.

Taking the job of data protection coordinator to prove that I could do things outside dental work. It was useful PR for me, although on reflection I don't think I did it well.

What advice would you give to someone aspiring to get a job like yours?

It will depend where you are coming from. For someone inside the service you need to have a job where you are enabled to show strength in your department that is perceived – it's the perception that is more important – to be well-managed.

To seek any opportunity in their own district to broaden their horizons. To find an area to get involved in outside their own specialty. This will bring them in touch with different kinds of people, which is important for their own learning, and later for their career.

To publish what they have done in some form in one of the health journals and to be able to take criticism from their peers.

To read journals about management in the health service, including the gossip, and to be prepared to quote from what they have read. It is inexcusable to be ignorant of what is happening in the NHS if you are seeking promotion within it. I have yet to go to an interview for any post in which I have not been asked such questions.

OTHER POINTS

I have a very strong feeling of uncertainty and occasionally wake up as if from a nightmare of being found out. When I worked as a dentist my skills were very clear: now that I am a manager, what is it that I do day-to-day that is distinctive? As a dentist I worked, now I don't feel that I do. I am not quite sure that what I am doing is genuine, hence the fear of being found out and made to work for a living! I would not describe what I am doing as hard work. I would like to become a DGM as the more 'political' less operational aspects of that role appeals greatly to me.

USING THIS CASE STUDY

Ask yourself the following questions:

1. What is most distinctive about what Mike says?
2. Are there any lessons for you in planning your career?
3. Are there any other lessons in his account?

10 The Twin Aspects of Leadership: Case Study 4 (Case Study of a DGM)

The aims of this case study are to illustrate two key aspects of leadership and many of the subjects discussed earlier.

Case Study 4 focuses on how this DGM saw his leadership role and how others saw him, rather than on the goals that he was seeking to achieve. This Case Study is very different from those in Chapter 9, which were based on a single interview, because it is an in-depth study deriving from the Templeton tracer study of DGMs. Peter Lawrence (a pseudonym) was a member of that study and was the subject of a case study written for NHSTA. This chapter uses some of the material from that Case Study – which was much more about the issues with which Peter was involved – but also draws on a later long interview with Peter on the subject of leadership. Frequent discussions were held with him over two years and four months and all his principal contacts were interviewed, some of them more than once. Their comments about him form part of this case. The DGM and his secretary also supplied a weekly record of his activities and contacts over two years.

BACKGROUND INFORMATION

The district

It is a medium sized district in an expanding area. There is a concentration of services on one site on the edge of a town, and one other main area of services in another part of the district. All the main health services are provided and there is a new district general hospital. The district is fortunate in its land assets.

The DGM

He is in his late 40s and has spent his working life in health service administration. He was previously the DA in the same district, which post he had held since the late 1970s. Before then the district had been known for its staff problems. When Peter became DGM the district was operating successfully.

GUIDELINES FOR ACTION IN THE EARLY DAYS

All the DGMs in the tracer study were asked about these. Peter was one of the few who found it easy to answer. These were his guides in the early days of the Griffiths reorganisation:

1. In carrying out the reorganisation, to be radical in a conservative guise by retaining titles but changing content.
2. To build on the good relationships that he had established as DA.
3. Concern for individuals so that in the reorganisation jobs were matched to people and no-one was jettisoned; to use existing managers but to change their approach to management. Only one new person was brought in and that only when the CNO decided to take early retirement.
4. To pick up the Griffiths ideas and sell them hard, explaining why with general management there had to be changes; particularly continuing the process of devolution started earlier.
5. To set objectives and measure progress against them. He attached great importance to this, so that a regular process of reviewing his subordinates against objectives was instituted from the early days.
6. The importance of publicising to the community what the district is doing, producing an annual report for this purpose, and of making the organisation sensitive and receptive to the public's opinions.
7. Advising DHA members about objectives and target dates so that they knew what to expect, and how to assess progress.

He described his task in the early days as follows:

'I've got to use one cohort of existing managers to help me change others because I can't relate to everybody myself . . . it's a bit like the New Testament, I am trying to convert my disciples to my aims and then I've got to send them out to preach to the rest, and changing them round is quite difficult – that is the biggest constraint.'

He also spoke of one of the most difficult and necessary tasks for a leader in a time of change – and that is when leadership is most necessary:

'To keep on an even keel in times of change and to present to the DHA and to the outside world a confident and stable facade.'

WHAT OTHERS EXPECTED OF THE DGM

The most common expectations were:

1. *Support*, particularly when times are difficult, 'so that I know that I can go ahead with what we have agreed with the confidence of his support'.
2. *Clear indication of priorities* for my work and of how he sees the district going.
3. *Minimum interference* 'that he trusts me to get on with the job without leaning over my shoulder'.

A variety of other expectations were mentioned by senior staff, thinking about their relationship with him, including:

- positive leadership;
- to be honest with me, but tactful;
- regular contact and to be available when help is needed;
- never to get angry;
- to treat me with respect;
- professional guidance, and expertise in areas where I am ignorant;
- that his expectations of me will be reasonable.

In the main, those interviewed said that Peter met their expectations.
  The chairman and vice-chairman had different kinds of expectations, which Peter also met:

'To be right in there at the patient interface. To be much more involved than as DA in ensuring that clinical practice was the most efficient we could attain, and in questioning clinicians on why they do what they do and on how they organise things.'

'That the buck should stop with him.'

PETER'S VIEWS ON LEADERSHIP

What is leadership?

Leadership is being high profile: shaping the choices and the priorities. Putting the decisions up in a way that cannot be avoided, and yet recognising that there are times when you have to bow to the inevitable and will not get what you want.

It is being confident in yourself and in your own evaluation and decision-making process.

There are two halves to it: expressing yourself, showing the district what you are and where you are going; and relating to those people who want to follow you.

Leadership is very personal. It is partially to do with status in the organisation, but it is much more than that. It is almost charismatic. It is you using yourself and your attributes and quite consciously sometimes. (One of the young leaders in Chapter 9, the medical UGM, said something similar: 'I just fish out of the hat for the different qualities I have and try and gear them to the situation at hand'.)

There are all sorts of roles in which you have to be the leader. Outside the district as representative spokesman, willy nilly you have become a public figure and are asked to speak on all sorts of occasions.

The two halves of leadership

I am quite fascinated by military views; if you read Mountbatten, Montgomery or Wellington, all tremendous leaders, they have the same two qualities. First, they are quite sure where they are going, and they mostly have the political skill to sell it. Second, they relate to the troops at any and every level on a personal basis. What they are doing, what you are doing, is saying: 'Yes, I am the leader, but all the time I am recognising you for your worth and what you are'. It is what I am very conscious of doing when I chair the joint consultative committee.

1. *Expressing yourself* – My sort of leadership is to do with me. Usually I would see it as me at the apex of the arrow, pushing at the centre. So you have to know what you are about. You have to be reasonably clear on your own directions.

2. *Relating to others* – You must recognise them as individuals; afford them room to grow and to express disagreement. You should get on to a basis where they acknowledge your leadership without feeling dominated by it.

In leadership in relation to the health authority and to the consultants I apply the same principles, but in a slightly more subtle way because there is no line relationship. With both these groups it is very important that you know what your goals are and that, generally speaking, it is clear to them what you are about. In seeking to get the health authority members to follow my lead, and in trying to encourage the consultants in the same way, I am trying to establish a personal relationship with each of them.

I pay a lot of attention to what the members want. If they ever ask me for anything, I go to some trouble to respond. I am saying to them very strongly: 'I see you as an individual and I want to listen to what you have got to say and to recognise your concerns'. That does not inhibit me from disagreeing with them, particularly in the formal situation, and relying on the strength of the relationship to carry you through a difficult period. Part of the leadership of members, who are fairly average people, is to treat them as equals and sometimes to defer to them while I think both parties realise that probably the general manager is dominant.

The same principles apply with my general managers. I am sometimes asked whether I have disagreements with them. Of course, I have quite sharp disagreements. There are occasions when you know there is an issue that you cannot afford to lose, so you want to dominate and to win it. But you hope that the strength of the relationship, its personal nature and the feel of the target that you are after, will carry you through such disagreements.

I could reckon to carry that through with the general managers and with the members, but I could not always do that with the consultant body. There will be times when they reject me and my leadership, then I have to fall back on other devices to get what I want.

Then there are the public occasions like a retirement party, when I am adopting the same approach to leadership. I am talking both to the person retiring and to the others, spreading some messages, increasing the understanding between all of us. I think of Mountbatten going round the South-east Asian Command and jumping on top of the Land Rover and having that ability to communicate to up to 500 and get it across.

Other aspects of leadership

3.   *Sharing leadership* – Another interesting aspect of leadership – and I am not quite sure that I fully understand it – is that most of the time you need to be clear and confident, but there are occasions when you need not be. There are times when you can step back a bit from the role and let other people share in it. I presume it is like hot and cold baths, you take people from one extreme to another: from feeling that they see you as the leader and feeling that they are sharing your leadership if only in a limited way. It is quite flattering as long, of course, as they do not have to share all the burdens that go with it. You make some space for other people, as in our away days.

Now that I am feeling a little more secure as the leader, I am happier to allow other people to have a prominent role in some situations. I think, like being on television, the Authority can get tired of always being presented with the same face. You know, it's Terry Wogan three times a week, we will go off you. So you can allow other people to lead on some things. Obviously people find that satisfying because they get the chance to shine individually and that varies the presentation and the feel of the organisation.

4.   *Bow down occasionally* – One special characteristic of leadership in the NHS is that though you are the leader, the head of the arrow, you have to accept that there are times when you are going to be humbled, not humiliated, but humbled. You cannot win everything and to do so would be bad policy. Sometimes you just have to recognise you will be defeated and be sensible and live with that; sometimes you can arrange little defeats or concessions. People like a leader; they like the strength and the reliability of somebody who knows his own mind. At the same time they will resent somebody who is infallible, or somebody who thinks he is. So, as well as drawing back to let other people share the leadership, you should accept defeats, and accept them ruefully, acknowledging: 'well, I lost that one'.

That is important with the chairman. There are some situations which I can concede to him, and one or two where he has been right and I have been wrong, but there are many others where I will step back and say: 'you are probably right there' or go back and say: 'I have thought about it and yes, that is the best way of doing it'. So you are bowing down a bit. And occasionally, of course, with your own subordinates too.

5. *The team* – Recollecting what I have said, I have not used the word 'team' once. Leadership is not without other individuals, but leadership is one individual. Others will contribute but a team does not lead. The team is there, but they are very much my team – how possessive I feel about my managers!

6. *Dangers of leadership* – Megalomania is quite a danger. If you are a leader as I have been describing it, then your big stumbling block is that you start to think that you are always right. That is encouraged because you get lots of toadies creeping round you because you are the boss, and you have to distinguish them from those who quite genuinely have something different to say that you ought to listen to.

You need a recognition of people's legitimate points of view. Listening to other people's criticisms is very important. It is not always easy, but if you are patient about it you can let other people's contribution influence the way you shape things. I am sometimes irritated by the advice that I get because it will slow down what I want to get done, but I have to recognise that I need to listen.

There is a balance needed: if you listen too much you get paralysed. You start to worry about your own values. If you lose self-confidence you are a dead duck, but if you allow self-confidence to become megalomania then you are also a dead duck.

HOW HE LEADS, AS SEEN BY HIS MAIN CONTACTS

By being a very distinctive personality:

'His personal strengths are that he is educated, has a sharp intelligence, a strong individual personality, a unique identity as a person, a very strong sense of humour, a positive leader with a lot of charisma.'

By being passionately, emotionally, committed to the NHS:

> 'He believes in the business that we are in . . . sometimes some of us get involved in the technicalities and he's likely to say: "come on there's a group of people out there, that's what it is about".'

> 'He has the patient in mind all the time and everthing that he does is related to that; he wants everybody else to be better motivated to accomplish that idea and is upset if they are not.'

One of his greatest strengths was seen to be his capacity to relate to other people:

> 'In those instances of excellent management that I have met, every employee feels that the manager has his eye on them. And however many levels there are between them and the manager at the top, they leapfrog those and relate psychologically to the man at the top. I think Peter has that ability.'

> 'Comparing him with other managers in the region, he's by far the most outgoing. So it makes it fairly easy to get rapport and, of course, there are the ties. It's part of the image. It's helpful because we are trying to change the image of the organisation and anything that projects humanity rather than process is helpful . . . It is the willingness to make oneself personally identifiable'.

> 'One of Peter's distinctive methods of managing is his friendliness and his ability to know the names even of the most junior members of staff.'

He knows what is going on:

> 'He works in an informal roving way. I have to be well informed of what is happening in my unit otherwise he finds out before I do.'

Another strength is his persuasive ability:

> 'He's a superb persuader.'

> 'His very skilled way of presenting demands, setting out his instructions very clearly and explaining the context.'

He is decisive and supportive:

> 'If you go to him for advice he will quickly decide, and if you have a problem he won't fob you off. I feel part of a team. I like, too, that if he has confidence in you he delegates to you and does not look

over your shoulder. But I also feel that he is available when I need him.'

His trustworthiness is important:

'He has a lot of integrity, I trust him . . . I know if it gets rough he will support me, he won't back off at the last moment and leave me exposed.'

He provides stimulus:

'There's a lot going on, it's a lively place. He's very innovative; he stimulates people; he's very supportive; he's very flexible. You can get an answer quickly and he'll let you do something different . . . It's very rarely that you get something back with a "no", that's why I say he's easy to work for. Very receptive to ideas and to using people in different ways.'

His intellectual abilities are admired:

'He's got an enormous capacity to keep close to a fair amount of detail across a very, very wide range, paradoxically he's also extremely good at seeing the wood for the trees.'

'His superb speech, his accurate use of words, and he can be moving on occasions at a farewell do.'

Two criticisms made of his leadership were that he can expect too much and criticise too readily:

'There is a world of difference if somebody says to me "I am disappointed but I realise you are trying very hard" or "I am disappointed why don't you try harder".'

And that he sometimes criticised someone in front of others.

LEADING IN DIFFERENT RELATIONSHIPS

This section describes Peter's aims and actions in dealing with the relationships in the different aspects of his job.

Relationships with the chairman

Peter had the same chairman throughout the study period. Both he and the chairman saw their relationship as a very important one.

Peter thinks that it is essential for a DGM to make sure of having the chairman's support, particularly on contentious issues.

His actions helped to shape his chairman's role. He thought a lot about how to make the relationship an effective one, as he did about all his major relationships. Even so, in the final interview he said:

'I think I have probably undervalued him for a long time, I am beginning to see his value and his strengths and perhaps if I had been a bit quicker about seeing how he and I fitted together in management terms, I would have been able to make more use of the balance that we have.'

(In the tracer study we noticed that many of the DGMs tended to undervalue their chairmen.)

Over the period Peter and his chairman learnt to work even better together, as the latter said:

'We have learnt to be frank with each other without taking offence.'

A DHSS observer at a meeting said to the chairman afterwards:

'it is remarkable how well you and the DGM gell, so that you each come in as appropriate'.

Relationships with the DHA

Peter sees the members' role being to challenge policy put to them. He said that he wanted to make them feel that they can make a positive impact without raising their expectations too much about what they can do. He ran a one day seminar to help them to explore what role they should play.

The vice-chairman described Peter as being always helpful and available to members, and having, via his director of education, launched a programme to help members with their role on mental health appeals and disciplinary appeals. He also said:

'Peter is good in being quite willing and capable of defending his officers against members when they criticise unfairly.'

Relationship with CHC

The CHC secretary said:

'His approach has not changed over time. When he first arrived he said to me: "we are going to have some unpalatable things to say to each other, so let's establish a good working relationship".'

'CHC members appreciate Peter because he does take the trouble to explain the decisions as do the other officers. They appreciate, too, the fact that he considers the CHC to be important and will listen to what they say. When they ask for something it's dealt with whether it is trivial or important.'

Peter has seen the CHC as part of the consumer network to which he attaches considerable importance. One of his aims is to empower the customer.

Relationship with UGMs

Three of the UGMs are on the same site and one in another part of the district. All four worked in the district before their appointments as UGMs, though one returned to the district to take up the appointment.

Peter has always attached great importance to the role of the UGMs, and he and the chairman toasted them in champagne when they were first appointed to mark their special status. He saw them as the main way of effecting change in the district. He is a strong believer in decentralisation. One of the UGMs explained how this operated in planning:

'In the past nine-tenths of the planning for units was done at district, and only the day-to-day issues at units. From my point of view the key to having a UGM is to look ahead, to plan for the future. Because of that we are doing things we would not have dreamt of three or four years ago.'

Peter uses a variety of different ways of communicating with the UGMs, he sees each of them regularly on their own for an hour to an hour and a half, about once a fortnight or once a month. These start by the UGM briefing him on what is going on and raising anything that he or she wants to. Then Peter 'chases me on any issues that he's concerned about and raises general issues'. There are also informal contacts when needed, but these are infrequent. There is a debriefing session for the UGMs after the DHA. About once every four months there is a meeting of the general managers with the treasurer, who is the deputy DGM, and the chief nurse, who is in charge of all training. This meeting was described by one UGM as a very useful way of keeping them together and stopping them being too parochially focused on their own unit. The UGMs are also full members of the successor to the DMT: Peter insisted on this, despite strong opposition from the consultant body.

Relationship with district managers

Peter adopts a similar approach to communication with the district managers, though adapted to their roles, personalities and location – the DMO's office is nearby so there are more brief personal contacts. He is actively involved in guiding, monitoring and encouraging the work of all the district managers, taking a particularly active interest in planning, and improving quality and the standard of nursing education.

He coordinates by means of informal meetings in his office. If there are any problems between individual managers he will try to sort it out informally. This may be one reason why there is little friction between UGMs and district managers. He also went to considerable trouble to clarify the responsibility of district managers: they are his managerial subordinates but their professional status is recognised by their direct access to him.

Relations with consultants

Peter was one of the most active of the tracer DGMs in seeking to involve consultants in management, in tackling any consultant who he judged not to be fulfilling his contract, and in trying to ensure that behaviour that was detrimental for patients was tackled by the representative consultants. He saw his role as general manager as having given him more power than he had before to influence consultants' behaviour.

He spent more time with consultants than most of the other DGMs in the tracer study. He sought to involve them in management in a wide variety of ways: clinical budgeting, persuading a consultant to chair a working party on information, and having regular meetings with the chairman of the MEC and the consultant on the district management group together with the chairman of the district.

Peter described what he was trying to do in his early period as DGM:

'I have been trying with help from one or two of the consultants to avoid getting hooked on big groups and principles, in discussing how far things go in a hypothetical situation and trying to relate it to practical situations where I think you can show by your attitudes towards a particular problem, a particular line of policy, that you can be decisive and questioning but realistic and accommodating at the same time.'

He worked with the relevant consultants, together with the UGM concerned, on changes to improve particular services, for example, one of the consultants, who though critical of general management, said:

'A lot of good work has been done on orthopaedics. That's a very solid achievement, an achievement of general management: an achievement because of the amount of political will tackling an issue that had been going on a long time.'

One comment about his personal approach to consultants was:

'I think he acts as a focus for the consultants' anxieties. They will ring him up at a moment's notice and he is very good about seeing them. I believe they rely on him much more than they would admit as an outlet for their anxieties. I think that is still true now there are UGMs.'

RGM and other regional managers

Peter has strong views about the role of region in relation to districts. He became the self-appointed spokesman for DGMs in his region in campaigning, successfully, for DGMs to have a much greater role in shaping the subjects to be discussed at the regular meetings with the RGM. He has also been active in trying to improve the regional review of the district and has got agreement to joint meetings beforehand to ensure thorough preparation. He feels that he has made the district review a positive one, which is beneficial to the district while satisfying the region.

Social services

One of Peter's various external activities was seeking to develop more satisfactory arrangements in his county for joint planning. In this he was successful. His chairman commented:

'He chairs the joint planning team and has good relationships. It was quite a struggle but now everybody's very pleased with it.'

Other district staff

The arts coordinator and the chaplain were two unexpected recurrent entries in the DGM's diary record. Both illustrate the importance that the DGM attached to the ambience within which patients are treated and staff work.

The job of the arts coordinator is to make environmental improvements inside and outside the group of hospitals on the main site. Currently she has a dozen projects for which she has to raise outside finance. She says:

'I tell him what I am doing. He is very well-informed and passionately interested.'

Peter and the chaplain meet once a quarter to review what the chaplain has learnt in the district. He thus provides Peter with another source of information about attitudes in the district and Peter feels he gains by sharing some current issues with him. The chaplain says that:

'Peter is always very supportive, particularly about training, and always positive about exploring ideas.'

LESSONS FOR OTHERS AS DESCRIBED BY HIS SENIOR STAFF

We asked those interviewed what lessons they thought Peter's approach to the job had for others. The main points made are given below:

- his accessibility and approachability;
- getting around and meeting people at all levels;
- being easily identifiable;
- his willingness to take risks: 'who dares, wins';
- allowing himself to be personally vulnerable;
- trusting his subordinates;
- trying to involve the CHC and the JCC very closely;
- using people creatively when a task appears: 'nurses as floor managers, doctors more involved in management, a laundry manager selling 2 million pounds of estates'.

WHAT PETER HAS LEARNT

Described by others

'To be a forceful manager and not to tolerate inefficiency in others.'

'He has changed and is still changing. He is becoming less isolationist, much more thoughtful about the repercussions of what he does outside.'

'To be more tolerant and patient.'

'He worries less and achieves more.'

'He manages his work so that he can get through a great pile without worrying that it will overflow.'

Described by himself

'I have learnt a lot about the health service in the context of the wider world . . . I have been surprised, I think, at the amount that I have learnt.'

'I have learnt a lot about how doctors behave and why they behave as they do. I feel I have had to learn to understand why it is so difficult.'

'I have learnt a lot more how to use, in a positive sense, my power within and outside the organisation, how to use one's position as "the boss" to change things.'

'and more personally, a lot about myself and the enormous presures and stress of the job.'

He commented in the final interview:

'The job is also a lot of fun; the trouble is when we have these discussions it always comes out sounding very serious and intense, but there is a lot of fun . . . and there is the power, the creative side of getting the organisation to address issues of what you can do for individuals, patients and staff, in the way you can put issues on the agenda and really get them debated, get them taken seriously, get them changed; that, if anything, has been a wider influence and a wider amount of power than I thought at the start.'

This should be an encouragement to readers to become a leader and to aim for general management!

MAKING USE OF THIS CASE STUDY

Ask yourself the following questions or use them as the basis for a group discussion of the case study:

1. What do you think is most distinctive about Peter as a leader? What else is distinctive?
2. What do you agree with in Peter's approach to leadership?
3. Are there any lessons for you? If yes, what? What are you going to do about it/them?
4. Is there anything you disagree with, or have reservations about? If yes, what and why?

More generally:

5. What are the main lessons about leadership in this case study?
6. What have you learnt about the job of a DGM by reading this case study?

Part IV

Developing Yourself

Part I discussed the nature of leadership. Part II sought to help you to lead more effectively in different kinds of relationships. Part III illustrated leadership in action. In Part IV, it is time for you to *think about yourself*. You will be a more effective leader if you understand, manage and develop yourself well. Chapters 11 and 12 seek to help you to do so.

11 Managing the Job and Yourself

'The management of self is critical. Without it, leaders may do more harm than good.' (Bennis and Nanus)[1]

Two essential aspects of being an effective leader are first, understanding and managing *yourself* and second, understanding and managing *your job*. This chapter draws on what others have learnt, including the DGMs who took part in the tracer study, to try and help you to do both. So it is intended as practical guidance and not as a psychological account.

THE IDEAL

Understanding and Managing Yourself

1. You develop **appropriate self-confidence in your ability to cope**, and have a realistic recognition of when you need help or should try to get somebody else to lead. It is better to err in being somewhat too confident, rather than too doubtful of your abilities.
2. You recognise your **strengths and weaknesses** in knowledge, understanding and skill.
3. You know how **wide or narrow is your understanding of other people**, and other professional groups, so that you can tell when you can trust your own judgement of others.
4. You **understand how you work**: what aspects of a job you tend to concentrate upon, and what you are likely to neglect or give too little attention to.
5. You can recognise **your own stress symptoms**, and have the sense to take them seriously and to do something about them.
6. You are aware of what you **still need to learn**. The leaders in Case Studies 1–3 had very different views on their learning needs, which can be used as a guide to thinking about your own learning needs.

Understanding the Job

1. You have a realistic view of the **scope of the job**, recognise its potential and the factors that constrain you.
2. You can assess what is good within your area of responsibility and **needs maintaining**, and what **needs changing**.
3. You can assess the **nature and amount of the resources available** to you.
4. You have identified the **key relationships**.

And Being Effective in it

1. You know **what you are trying to achieve**. You are alert to potential threats to what you are doing, and want to do, and active in trying to forestall them. You notice and use opportunities that arise to further your aims.
2. You are able to **prioritise your work** and, unless there is good reason not to, to keep to your priorities.
3. You have the **self-discipline to tackle difficult decisions** and, as Alan says in Case Study 2:

   'Be ruthless with yourself, and make that demonstrable, in never allowing things to be fudged – unless by conscious decision.'

4. You can both take a **broad view** of the factors relevant to a particular problem and, when necessary, understand the **details**.
5. You can prevent yourself getting too immersed in **operational detail** and **too attracted by 'firefighting'**.
6. You are aware of the danger of **spending too much time working in areas that you enjoy**, particularly those that really belong to an earlier job – your play area(s) – and exercise the necessary self-discipline.
7. You seek to increase your understanding of all those whose **cooperation you need**.
8. You can **manage your time efficiently**. It is an essential ability in very busy jobs, but it is not the most important aspect of managing yourself.

There are, of course, many other factors that are relevant to effectiveness. Some of these are aspects of leadership discussed earlier in this book. The ones described above are aspects of managing your job that you could reasonably set yourself as ideals, because they should be obtainable by people with very different personalities.

DIFFICULTIES IN ACHIEVING THE IDEAL

The main difficulties in managing yourself come, not surprisingly, *from yourself*, but there may also be difficulties inherent in the job and the particular situation within which you work.

Difficulties From Yourself

Some people learn the *self-discipline* that is needed to be an effective leader early in life; others have painfully to acquire it.

Some people are much *better organised* than others. Others have a struggle to learn to keep on top of the varied demands of their job.

A common difficulty in more senior jobs is a continuing attraction to *operational details*, and the enjoyment of *'firefighting'*.

Some people have a greater capacity for *objectivity* than others. Leaders need to combine commitment – preferably passionate commitment – to the ideal, to the vision of how the organisation for which they are responsible should change, with a capacity for detached analysis of the situation. This is a hard combination, but the first is more important than the second and the second is easier to learn.

The *level of energy and drive, as well as ambition*, differs between individuals, but if you are, or are aspiring to be, a leader you will need to be well above average on all three, though ambition need not be personal – it can be ambition for the achievements of your group.

Too great an opinion of the *importance of your own contribution* compared with that of others makes it hard for you to manage, as that is likely to mean that you do too much and delegate too little. Too much misplaced confidence in your managerial abilities is also dangerous – doctors may be more likely than those from other backgrounds to overrate their knowledge and skill in managing.

Conversely, *too little confidence* will make it hard for you to be accepted as a leader.

Difficulties in the Job and its Situation

Some jobs require greater abilities for *self-management* than others. A barrage of difficult and demanding problems make it hard to organise your time and to give attention to other important but less immediately pressing problems. Many of the DGMs in the tracer study found that it was difficult to cope with the volume of work in their new jobs: the amount of paper to be read and processed, the number of people to be seen and the variety of problems to be tackled. Nor was this a temporary phenomenon, though it was worst in the early days. So it is hard to manage oneself in tough and demanding jobs. Heather-Jane also talked about the difficulties of managing your time in a demanding job.

Some jobs are *inherently more stressful* than others, though the sources of stress vary. Inadequate support at work and at home can make a great difference to the ease with which you can cope.

One or more of the *key relationships* may be specially difficult. In many jobs, the character of your boss makes a considerable difference to the ease with which you can manage yourself. This is particularly true for a DGM's relationship with the chairman.

So there are real difficulties in the situation, but however difficult it is you can *help yourself*.

STEPS TOWARDS THE IDEAL

Understanding and Managing Yourself

1. *Developing self-confidence* – The importance of self-confidence is discussed by the young leaders in Chapter 9 and in Case Study 1. Several said that they sought to display self-confidence even if 'they were quaking inside'. The tracer DGMs in their final interview often talked about how they had developed self-confidence and how much easier this made it for them.

   A problem for many who get to the top of their particular part of the organisation is being *alone up front*, as one of the DGMs said:

   > 'At work I have never been anything other than a team member before. I have had to relearn the sort of confidence that I used to have at school when I was captain of sports teams and so on. It's relearning the confidence to be on one's own.'

   Self-confidence about your ability to do your job should come with more *experience of working in it*. It is the more general self-confidence that many younger leaders need to develop. Seeking opportunities for public speaking, even taking a course on public speaking, is a way of gaining confidence on your feet. Taking leadership positions in outside organisations, whether professional bodies, voluntary organisations or sports is another way of developing your confidence and widening your experience of human nature.

The mature and more senior leader may have to use other means of developing or at least sustaining confidence. A counsellor, confidante or guru, whichever is your inclination and you can find, is someone that most leaders need and with whom they can share and examine their doubts. The burden of appearing confident when you are not may otherwise be too heavy.

2. *Avoiding over-confidence* – The section headed 'megalomania' in Peter's account in Case Study 4 is a good warning of this danger. You need to have – and to retain – a capacity to listen to critical comments.

3. *Understanding and managing your stress* – This is one of the most essential abilities for any leader in a difficult and demanding job. The first step is recognising when you are getting too stressed, because the common and dangerous pattern is to deny the stress or to work even harder because you feel you are not coping. A symptom of stress is the belief that you are indispensable!

Individuals have their own stress symptoms: the more common ones are sleeping badly, indigestion and, more for women, tearfulness. Learn to recognise your own and to take heed. Learn, too, what stresses you and try to avoid it if you can, or else try to take some recuperative action afterwards. One of the tracer DGMs commented on this recognition of what was personally stressful:

> 'I have learnt a lot about getting over-stressed, what stresses me and how to avoid it. For example, I realise that having a backlog of work is the worst thing. I get really stressed if I have not read the paperwork for a meeting . . . I have got to keep up with all the issues, so if I take time off, which people advise me to do, then it actually makes things worse . . . I have also realised that I simply must have seven hours sleep at least five nights a week. And I have also cut down on drinking when I am stressed.'

A good manager absorbs the stress so none is passed down to workers under them.

You also need to learn what *relaxes you*, and try to ensure that you get the relaxation you need; competitive sport may not be a good relaxation when you are feeling stressed. There are various sources of help for stress: books, relaxation classes and tapes and individual counselling.

Use the ideal for understanding and managing yourself as a checklist to see whether you need to improve. If so, use Chapter 12 as a guide to *developing yourself*.

Understanding the Job and Being More Effective in it

All except the best organised managers need to lift themselves occasionally out of their immersion in immediate tasks and problems, to take stock of *what they are doing*. This section aims to help you to think about the *nature* of your job and the *scope* that you have to realise your vision. It provides different ideas and models for thinking about how you tackle your job. They have all been used by other managers and found helpful. However, individuals differ, so that you are likely to find some of them more illuminating than others.

Managers vary in how they *learn*: some are analytical and can easily learn by reading and reflection; some are very practical and learn mainly by doing and finding out whether it works or not. Most managers are in between: they are primarily practical in their approach to their job, but do welcome learning of new ways of understanding their situation so that they can control it better. This section is addressed to the latter group as well as to the analytical manager.

1. *Demands, constraints and choices* – Job descriptions can, at best, give only a very limited picture of a job. They do not capture the reality of a changing situation, the complexity of relations with individuals and groups, nor the scope that exists for jobholders to concentrate on particular aspects of the job. So each jobholder has to discover what the job is like. This is a personal discovery, as shown by the great variations in the kind of work that is done by people in similar jobs. People do jobs differently because their abilities vary, but also because they see different things as being important, interesting or enjoyable. They notice different things, as anyone following managers in similar jobs who are doing a tour of the workplace will soon discover.

These variations in what people in similar jobs can do mean that **managerial jobs offer considerable scope for individuals to choose what they do**. Two jobholders can focus their attention on different parts of the job. One, for example, may mainly concentrate on subordinates and the work that they are doing, while another may spend most of the time on working with people outside his or her own command. The model of demands, constraints and choices in Figure 11.1 provides a graphic way of thinking about how you can best use the opportunities that exist in your job to decide what work you think is *most important*.

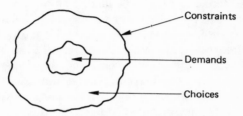

Figure 11.1   Model of a job: demands, constraints and choices

Figure 11.1 show the *core of the job*, labelled 'demands' – that is, the work that anyone in the job would have to do, because they could not survive in the job unless it was done. These are the tasks that you *cannot neglect or delegate*. Figure 11.1 also shows an outer boundary of *constraints*, that *limit* what the jobholder can do, and an area of *choices* that is the work that one person in the job may do and another may not. One DGM, for example, may choose to take a great deal of interest in what is happening in mental handicap, another may leave that almost wholly to the unit general manager; one DGM may spend almost all the time within the district, another may spend one or two days a week away on regional, national or professional activities.

A major choice in all junior and middle management jobs – and even, to a lesser extent, in some senior ones – is how much time the manager spends in *operational work*, doing what he or she was originally trained to do. In the Case Studies, Heather-Jane is the only one who talks specifically about that, and the reasons for getting so involved.

The lines in Figure 11.1 are uneven, to indicate that all three parts of the diagram can change: a new boss may bring fresh demands, new constraints may appear, such as new legislation, or the manager may choose to try and reduce one of the constraints, such as attitudes opposing a change, and succeed in doing so. Changes in demands and in constraints can affect the *amount* and *nature* of the choices available. Different jobs will vary in how large or small is the core of demands, but in all there will be scope for choice. In general management jobs, there is a very large area of choice.

The choices that you exercise – though often you may not do so consciously – are what you *focus your attention upon*. One simple way of discovering this is how your time is divided between different categories of contacts. Figure 11.2 shows a way of thinking about whether you mainly choose to spend your time with your subordinates, and the relative time and attention you pay to relations with other departments – or, if you are a unit manager, with other units – compared with contacts with your boss and other more senior managers and with those outside the NHS.

People not only do jobs differently, they also see them differently. It can be liberating to recognise that how you see your job is very personal, and may impose quite unnecessary limitations upon what you can do. One manager, for example, will think that much more of the job consists of inescapable demands than will another who has a truer recognition of how much choice the job offers in practice.

Similarly, people in the same job may have a very different view of the constraints that limit what they can do. Some people feel hemmed in by constraints so that there is little they think they can do, whereas another person in the same job will see fewer constraints and seek to test troublesome constraints to see if they can be overcome. To quote John Harvey-Jones again:

> 'one of my personal invariable rules is that when I have mentally decided that something cannot be done, for what appears to be a very good reason, I test that apparent constraint, hopefully to destruction'.[2]

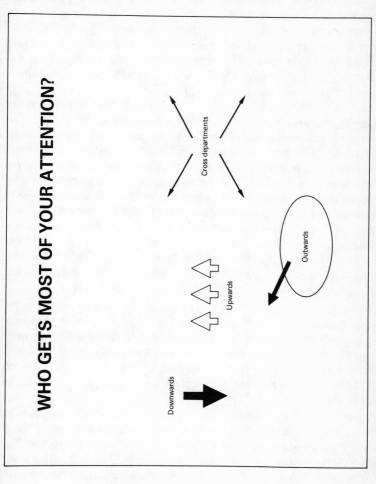

Figure 11.2　Who gets most of your attention?

The framework of demands, constraints and choices, which is described more fully in an earlier book by the author,[3] can help you in thinking about personal priorities: whether some of the work that you do is indeed a demand, that is work you *must* do, or really something that you have *chosen* to do. Recognising the latter can be particularly valuable when the volume of work presses heavily, because it can show you where you may be able to cut back. If you look back at your engagement book you can ask yourself how much of your work was really a demand, and if so who imposed it, was it yourself? If yourself, is this something that you think you should continue to do?

2. *Domain* – The area in Figure 11.1, which is bounded by the constraints line, shows the job's potential domain or *territory*. In practice, many jobholders occupy a smaller domain – that is their sphere of influence is smaller. One UGM, for example, does not seek to influence the DGM, or to play any part outside her own unit, whereas another may be actively interested in helping to shape district policies; one ward sister exercises considerable influence over the consultants who work there, whereas another accepts a subservient role. Managers with the narrower view – and, hence, smaller domain – are focusing their attention downwards, on subordinates, rather than sideways, upwards and outwards to all those whose actions and attitudes can affect their work and the resources available to them (see Figure 11.2).

    Most managerial jobs in the NHS offer jobholders some choice as to whom they seek to influence and in how wide an influence they try to have. **The idea of 'domain' is useful for stimulating you to think how wide an area you should be active in if you are to achieve your vision, and therefore who you should *seek to influence*.**

3. *Boundaries* – Your domain has a boundary, which in many jobs is partially flexible. Once you have decided how large you want your domain to be, you need to be sensitive to what is happening *at its periphery*. Are there threats to the boundary? If so, what can you do to forestall them? Alternatively, are there parts of the boundary that you want to extend, where you feel that a wider influence is necessary to achieve your goals?

    For many managers the boss is, at least at first, the most important person to influence, particularly if he or she is, in your opinion, unduly restrictive of your activities. UGMs, for example, may want to have a say in the formation of district policies to try and ensure that account is taken of the effects of such policies upon their unit. DGMs and UGMs have been forced by financial pressures, and their accountability for a balanced budget, to seek to influence decisions that the doctors had seen as within their domain.

Managers at any level may feel the need to *extend* their domain so that they can influence those outside their establishment who can help or hinder what they are trying to accomplish. Many managers in the NHS will seek to influence the policies and actions of the social services and the FPC in their district. Others will want to enlist the help of people in the community, just as members of the energy team in the Worthing hospital, described in Chapter 7, and Heather-Jane in Case Study 1, did to get help with their aim of making the daily lives of their elderly patients more interesting.

Thinking in terms of the boundary of your domain has another use, that of *identifying where there may be difficulties in relationships*. Organisation structures create separate departments and separate levels; in doing so, boundaries are created between one type of work and another. These clarify what kind of work is to be done and by whom. However, they also can easily create a feeling of 'we' and 'they', and hence of potential difficulties in relationships.

The ease with which people come to see some as 'we' and others as 'they' can be shown experimentally. In one evening a group of strangers divided into groups will come to identify with members of their own group and see the others as outsiders. Any manager planning a reorganisation should remember that where divisions are made, boundaries are created with dangers of misunderstanding, even distrust. Where there is such a danger, or where the 'we and they' attitude already exists, it is important to facilitate *informal contacts*. Such contacts usually encourage people to feel friendly.

So far, we have concentrated on understanding the nature of the job to help you to review how you do it. Now we turn to more specific ways in which you can seek to be more effective in your job.

4. *Time management* – The simplest place to start is with how you *actually spend your time*. Many people, studies suggest, have a distorted view of what they do, overestimating the time that they spend on some activities and underestimating that on others. So keep a running record of what you are doing for a week or more; if you have a secretary she can do much of it for you. Check this against what you *believe* you are doing and what you think you *ought to be* doing. The next stage is to check on how much time you are giving to particular activities or people, and whether you are *satisfied* with this. You may remember the quotation in Chapter 1 from Tom Peters on the need to show that you really think a subject is important by visibly spending a lot of time on it.

    A record of how you spend your time tells you about how you are dividing your time between different problems, activities and people. It enables you to ask yourself how much of the work you do *you judge to be important*. Such a record can also show you what the pattern of your day is like: Is it very fragmented? Are there lots of interruptions? How often do you interrupt yourself turning away from a difficult paper or problem? How much time do you spend in your office? How often do you visit? These are examples of some of the questions that you could usefully ask yourself about what you actually do. Many managers after keeping a record of how they spend their time decide that they ought to make some changes.

    The next step is to decide whether you need help or whether you can *discipline yourself* to make the necessary changes. Help comes in three main forms: courses on the management of time – their long-running popularity shows how common a problem it has always been; books;[4] and personal assistance. Many managers can make better use of their secretaries who often have more of a capacity to act as personal assistants than is recognised and some of whom have much more organising ability than their bosses! Many leaders need administrative help, even if they themselves have come from an administrative background. The ex-service recruits to general management brought with them an understanding of the importance of such staff support.

5. *Keeping in touch*[5] – It is common for senior managers over the

years to bemoan the fact that they do not spend enough time visiting their staff: a characteristic that was noted more than thirty years ago by Sune Carlson in a pioneering study of nine Swedish managing directors.[6] He also noted that they did less visiting than they thought. Several of the DGMs in the tracer study regretted that they did not find more time to visit, and vowed to do better in the future. It seems to be something that leaders say they believe is important but in practice give it too low a priority for them to spend much time on. Visiting is more important for a leader than for someone who is managing without also leading. Leaders have a greater need to be in touch with what their staff are thinking, and to be seen around 'spreading the messages' that they want to put across.

There are many other ways of keeping informed about what is happening, but few are substitutes for the wide informal personal contact that can be achieved by visiting your staff, especially if they are numerous and in different locations.

You should always be striving to have a better understanding of what people are really thinking. Srivastva and Barrett put it well:

'Organizations need to experiment continually with new ways to facilitate the expression of members' concerns and ideas and create processes that are occasions for discovery.'

They go on to suggest that:

'organizations need to create an "antiorganization", a "time-out" in which anyone is free to say anything, an arena where members are free to parody the formal organization and everyone agrees not to take offense . . . a chance to . . . create a parody of the official culture where members can laugh at their own conventions from a safe distance'.[7]

An opportunity that is sometimes taken in Christmas parties.

It is all too easy to think in a stereotyped way about listening to what your staff are really thinking and about how you get across your messages to them. The common description for both is 'good communications', but you need to *think creatively*, as Srivastva and Barrett suggest, about how you are really going to achieve that in practice.

Time management and keeping in touch have been highlighted as two important areas where it is easy for you to take action. Even more important is it for you to use the points listed under the ideal, at the beginning of this chapter, as a checklist for *reviewing where you need to improve*. Then you can go back to consider how effective a leader you are by reviewing yourself against the ideal in Chapter 1 and the ideal for your own relationships discussed in subsequent chapters.

SUMMARY

To be an effective leader you need to understand and manage *yourself*. You need also to understand your job and to be able to *appraise the way that you tackle it*.

1. *The ideal*

(a) *Understanding and managing yourself*:

- you develop *appropriate self-confidence*;
- you understand your *strengths and weaknesses*;
- you recognise how *wide or narrow is your ability to understand other people*;
- you understand *how you work*, particularly what aspects of the job you may overlook or ignore;
- you know when you are *too stressed*, and take action;
- you are aware of what you *still need to learn*.

(b) *Understanding the job and being effective in it*:

- you know what you are *trying to achieve*;
- you understand the *scope and nature* of your job, and the *key relationships*;
- you can *prioritise* your work successfully;
- you are *self-disciplined* and do not evade difficult decisions;
- you can take a *broad view* of problems but can, when necessary, understand the *detail*;
- you *manage your time* well;
- and, of course, you have the *social skills* needed for leading in your different relationships.

2. *Difficulties in achieving the ideal*
   There may, of course, be real difficulties in your situation – it

would not be a challenging job unless this was true – but many of the difficulties may come *from yourself*. These can include: lack of self-discipline and poor organisation; an attraction to work that should be done by your juniors; an inability to look at problems objectively; insufficient drive and energy or ambition for the achievement of your vision, and too little (or too much) self-confidence.

3. *Steps towards the ideal*

(a) *Understanding and managing yourself*:

–   you may need to develop, or to maintain, your self-confidence; it is less likely, but possible, that you will need to avoid *over-confidence*;
–   the more challenging your job, the more important it is that you understand and manage your *stress symptoms*;
–   use the ideal as a checklist to decide where you need to develop yourself.

(b) *Understanding your job*:

–   You will benefit from taking stock of *how you see your job*, and *how you are doing it*. Realise that your view of your job is a highly personal one; you see it differently from another job-holder. You are focusing your attention on particular aspects of the job, that is you are making choices – though you may only partly recognise this – in what you *do* and what you do *not do*. It helps to review the choices that you are making and ask yourself whether they are currently the right ones. You should also subject what you see as your main *constraints* to a stringent review, to check how real they are.
–   Consider the domain – that is, the territory, that you occupy – and whether you need to try and extend it if you are to realise your vision. Think of your domain as having a *boundary*: do you need to protect any of your boundaries? Do you need to establish closer relations with those on the edge of your boundary?

(c) *Being more effective in the job*:

–   improve your *time management* unless you are already very good at it;
–   keep *in touch* with your staff; strive to improve your understanding of what they really think; make time to visit;

- use the ideal as a checklist for asking yourself how close you are to the ideal; then turn to Chapter 12 to consider how you are going to *develop yourself*.

12 Developing Yourself

'*A new model of leadership that expresses an ethic of self-development is needed, not just at the top, but at all levels.*' (Michael Maccoby)[1]

'*Perception is the first step towards knowledge.*' (John Locke)

Nowadays leaders need to develop themselves, both as leaders and as managers, if they are to cope successfully with the changes affecting them. The aim of this chapter is to help you to think what this means, and how you can best develop yourself – it is not about professional updating.

We are all partially blind: blind to ourselves, to others and to what is happening around us. **Part of developing yourself is improving your perceptions. It is recognising what you did not see before. This is the most important – and the hardest – aspect of self-development. It is one where there is always more to learn.**

The DGMs in the tracer study discussed what they realised that they had learnt during their first two years in the job. Often this was about recognising *what they did not know*:

'to discover in mid-life that there are all these things that you thought you knew and actually don't . . . is quite a revelation'.[2]

'I have learned a lot about the health service in the context of the wider world . . . I have been surprised, I think, at the amount that I have learned. I had never thought I was a particularly naive person but I have seen a lot more complexity . . . than I had realised existed.'

'I, like most NHS chief officers and probably people in any discipline, made certain assumptions about my levels of understanding about the functions of other disciplines. I am now finding these assumptions were not terribly well founded so I need to spend time with my colleagues to make sure I understand enough of what their function is.'

'I have changed my approach to problems because I have learnt of the great gaps in my experience and I now seek out other perspectives more than I did.'

The experience of leadership teaches you about yourself, as one of the tracer DGMs described:

> 'What I have learned about myself and the enormous pressures and stress of the job has been an enormous amount.' (DGM)

The young leaders in Chapter 9, pp. 118–19, also discuss what they have learnt, including what they have learnt about themselves.

Experience can be a great teacher – but, like other forms of teaching, how much you learn depends *upon yourself*.

Self-development means taking responsibility for your own learning, and helping others to develop themselves.[3] The idea of self-development has been popular since the 1970s for the following reasons:

1. Recognition of the limitations of what can be accomplished by *traditional training programmes*.
2. More awareness of how people *differ* in personality, training and experience, and hence the need for more *individualised* development.
3. The trend towards *greater participation* and *personal autonomy*.
4. The economies of *do-it-yourself training*.
5. The development of training methods that make it easier for individuals *to learn on their own* via TV, videos and computers.
6. The need for individuals to *assume more responsibility for managing their own careers*, because of the decline in job security, and the greater mobility within and between organisations.

It is easy to think of learning too narrowly as just formal education, but it is much wider than that. It includes:

- *updating* knowledge;
- learning about *new subjects* and *techniques* that are relevant to your work;
- improving your skills, particularly your *social skills*;
- exploring *good practice elsewhere*;
- learning more about the *environment* within which you work;
- developing your understanding of the interests, attitudes and problems of the people who can *affect your job*;
- *understanding yourself better*, your strengths and weaknesses, and how your behaviour is seen by others; learning to manage yourself better.

THE IDEAL

That *you will*:

1. recognise the need for **continued learning**;
2. accept **responsibility for your own learning**;
3. recognise **how easy it is to get bogged down in your work**, particularly in immediate problems, and take steps to try and counteract this;
4. understand **what best stimulates you to learn**, and seek out such stimulus while trying to remain open to other ways of learning;
5. think broadly about what **'learning' means**;
6. learn from your **failures as well as your successes**.

You need to want to learn, and to *know how* to learn.

You should think broadly about what learning means so that you can make good use of all the varied opportunities that there are to do so. Some people show a greater capacity for learning from what happens to them than do others. The ideal is that you should be able to learn from your experiences.

DIFFICULTIES IN ACHIEVING THE IDEAL

Reading the ideal should immediately suggest some of the potential difficulties. There are four main ones:

1. Accepting that you *still need to learn*, and that you *can* still learn, even if you are experienced in your work and no longer young.
2. Thinking sufficiently broadly about learning: it is easy to accept that you need to learn a new technical skill for which you can see an immediate use, but harder to accept that *broadening your understanding* is a useful form of learning.
3. Accepting that learning is sufficiently important to *make time* both for formal learning and for activities that stimulate you to think afresh.
4. Not knowing how to learn: you may have too *narrow a learning repertoire* (this is explained below).

There may be other difficulties, too: you may have been too long in the same job to find it stimulating; you may have a heavy but unchallenging workload; you may work for a boss who you think constrains you unduly; no-one may have tried to help you to develop; or you may have reacted against your experience of management education, and you may have difficult home circumstances that restrict your ability to develop yourself outside working hours.

There are also potential difficulties for *your boss*, even if he or she is interested in management development. One is making time to think about, and try to contribute to, your development. Another difficulty is accepting the value of self-development in practice. It is alw ays a temptation to believe that one knows best what is good for other people.

There are fewer difficulties if you are young because you are more likely to accept that you need to learn, and others will be more aware that they should help you, and more motivated to do so.

STEPS TOWARDS THE IDEAL

The first step, at any age, is to *recognise the need to learn*

The most powerful motivation for learning is a *need to know*. This can be triggered by *failure*, which is why failure can be such a fruitful stimulus for learning unless it is explained away by rationalisations. If, for example, you did not get selected for a job that you wanted, ask yourself if the selectors may have been right not to choose you?

Another reason for needing to know is recognising a *gap between what you are and what you need to be* to fill your current or desired job satisfactorily. If you are satisfied with your own performance, you will see little need to learn. If so, your first step towards the ideal is to develop higher standards for your performance, and to recognise what you do not know. You may also need a more realistic assessment of your performance.

For the Young
1. **Seek to understand the kind of person that you are**: what are your strengths and weaknesses, what is distinctive about the way that you interpret what is happening and in how you relate to other people? There are a variety of personality tests, such as the Myers–Briggs,[4] that can help you, and a good many short programmes. Many companies run assessment centres that can be very helpful guides to your career potential, and so do some

regions in the NHS. If you want a do-it-yourself analysis a helpful book is Pedler, Burgoyne and Boydell, *A Manager's Guide to Self-Development.*[5]

2. **Consider what you can do to overcome, or at least to *lessen*, your weaknesses**, and consult whoever you find helpful about how to do this.

3. **Look for an older manager who can act as your guide** – now often called a mentor.

4. **There are many skills that a manager needs that can be improved by watching others** – for example, chairing; how to say 'no' without causing offence; how to organise your time; and how to make your expectations clear. So look out for people who are good at one or more of these skills, and study how they do it.

5. **Ask yourself who are the leaders**, or who show leadership abilities, in a particular situation? Why is it that others accept their leadership? **What can you learn from what they do?**

6. **Think about what you want from your career.** Review your qualifications and consider what others are necessary, or might be helpful, and plan how studying for these can be fitted in with your other commitments.

7. **Ask yourself what you are doing outside work that contributes to your development**, and whether you should consider doing more. Such rounded development is very much part of the 'university ideal', but the pressures of starting work, learning a new job and setting up a home can easily lead to a much narrower range of interests than at university – do-it-yourself around the house will not do much to develop you as a leader in the NHS, but active involvement in community work and team sports can give you opportunities to practise leadership skills. There may – probably should – be times when domestic commitments preclude external activities as well as a job, so you need to make good use of the time before and, when you are older, after your family has grown up.

8. **Consider going on a leadership development course**: there are many different kinds including those that test you in hard physical conditions. Weigh up the usefulness of such courses and be prepared to pay for yourself if you cannot get funded by any other source.

9. **Recognise what stimulates you to learn, but try to broaden the ways that you learn.** Kolb's[6] widely quoted classification of learning methods can help you to analyse how you learn. Kolb

argues that learning is a four stage process, but that people tend to be stronger at one or two stages and give inadequate attention to the others. The four stages are:

(a) Concrete experience (*doing*);
(b) Reflective observation (*reviewing*);
(c) Abstract concepts and generalisation (*analysing*);
(d) Active experimentation (*trying it out*).

The four stage learning model provides a way of thinking about how to widen your learning repertoire by practising the stages that you *tend to ignore*. Some people, for example, are weak at reflective observation so if they make a mistake or are unsuccessful in achieving one of their aims they do not reflect on why that has happened. Others analyse but do not try out their conclusions. The use of the four stages of learning is illustrated on p. 183.

For the Middle Work Years
1. Consider which of the suggestions for the young **should still apply to you**.
2. Now is a good time to **review your achievements against your expectations**, and to consider what you want from your future career. Developing yourself may be essential if you are planning a change of career, and will still be necessary if you expect to continue in the same way.
3. **This is often a good time to do something different, preferably a new job but if not that, then look for other ways of challenging yourself to think and act differently.** Particularly if you are in a senior management post, you will benefit from finding somebody who can test your arguments and help you to think of new approaches. If there is no-one you feel that you can use in that way in your district or region, then look for someone outside. Additionally, establish an information exchange with your opposite number in another district.
4. **Take part in some formal development activity each year,** whether it is a workshop, seminar, or course, but choose carefully. Aim to go to at least two, one to extend your knowledge of the health service and the other your knowledge of management. For the latter, widen your horizons by going, at least occasionally, to a programme that includes managers from outside the NHS.
5. Visit other districts or regions, if you work at region, and, if you

can, health services in other countries. Use such visits as a way of **consciously practising each part of the learning cycle**:

(a) concrete experience – *impressions of the visit*;
(b) reflective observation – *reviewing what you noticed*;
(c) generalisations – what could or could not be *applied here*, and why?;
(d) experimentation – *trying it out*.

For the Later Work Years

Suggestions 3–5 above apply equally to you, suggestion 3 is especially important. Taking a very different type of job is remarkably revivifying, as the experience of many older managers shows. Failing that, **you need, even more than those in their 40s, to find people who will challenge your views** – the reason for the court jester – and to **put yourself in new situations so that you are not too restricted to (and limited by) your customary ways of thinking and acting**.

For All

Reread the ideal and the common difficulties that may prevent you learning as much and as effectively as you could. **Recognise that**

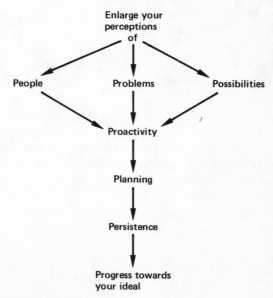

Figure 12.1 The 8p diagram

**learning is not just formally acquiring new knowledge and qualifica-
tions, or even seeking new job challenges, it is also very much trying to
enlarge your perceptions.** Hence the quotation from John Locke at
the head of this chapter. We are all in danger of tunnel vision, in the
way we see *problems*, *possibilities* and *people*. You should seek to
enlarge your *perceptions* of all three. Doing so will enhance your
leadership abilities. It will do so even more if you can ally these four
'Ps' with three others: *proactivity*, *planning* and *persistence*, so as to
progress your vision of the ideal. The sequence is shown in the 8P
diagram in Figure 12.1.

SUMMARY

You should seek to develop yourself throughout your career so that
you can lead and manage more effectively. You should *want* to learn,
and to improve your *ability to learn*.

1. The most important part of developing yourself is recognising
    what you do not know. There is always more to learn about:
    — the *context* within which you work;
    — the *jobs* of those you are trying to *lead*;
    — understanding *other people's* attitudes;
    — understanding *yourself*.

2. You should consciously *try to learn*, and to improve your *ability
    to learn*.

3. If you are young:
    — seek to *understand* your strengths and weaknesses, and *take
       action* to reduce your weaknesses;
    — look for *role models* both for how to lead and for specific skills;
    — plan what you should learn to meet your *career ambitions*;
    — seek out opportunities to *practise leadership*, both at work and in
       your leisure activities.

4. If you are no longer young:
    — do something *different*, preferably a new job, that challenges
       you;
    — take part every year in *formal development activities*;
    — visit other districts, regions, countries; *review* what you learn and
       apply it.

5. For all: *apply the 8P diagram*.

In Conclusion

The NHS needs leaders who can enthuse others with high goals for what they can achieve.

Do not have too grand an idea of leadership. You do not have to be charismatic but you must care – and care deeply – about what you want to achieve. You must show that you care in what you do because you are a model for other people's actions.

Think boldly about what you and your group, large or small, should be trying to achieve. If you call it a vision, that will encourage you to be bold. Enlist others in building that vision.

Set high standards, and exemplify them. Be positive, for positive thinking spreads. Encourage others and when you feel discouraged keep it to yourself, or better share it with a trusted counsellor.

Leadership means enlisting others as willing cooperators. To do that you must recognise their importance and show that you consider them and their work important. You must also understand why their views may differ from yours and seek to find common goals. Above all, you must inspire trust: that is a key aspect of successful leadership in the NHS because there are so many individuals and groups who may be suspicious of you and your intentions.

A good leader should also be an effective manager. You will not be effective unless you are able to understand and manage yourself and your job.

You have to be willing to pay the price of leadership: hard work, pressures, becoming tougher, handling the conflict – particularly in yourself, if you are clinically trained, between professional and managerial objectives – discouragement and loneliness. However, the price brings rewards, as you saw in the Case Studies in Part III, above all the feeling that you have made a difference. I hope that you will want to pay the price – or, if you are already doing so, that you have found some ideas and suggestions in this book to help you to lead even better.

Working for Patients proposes radical changes. These provide new opportunities for, and fresh challenges to, leadership. Use the three-step analysis of this book (ideal, difficulties in the way of its achievement and steps towards the ideal) to help you to be a good leader.

Appendix A

DETAILS OF THE TEMPLETON TRACER STUDY OF DGMs

This study was financed by the NHSTA from April 1985 to the end of September 1987. The study was initiated and directed by Rosemary Stewart. Professor Derek Williams was consultant to the project, Dr John Gabbay and Sue Dopson were the full-time research associates and Peter Smith, of Ashridge Management College and an Associate Fellow of Templeton College, was a part-time research associate. Val Martin was the secretary to the project.

The study had four aims:

1. To understand the job of the newly appointed district general managers.
2. To identify the strengths and weaknesses of different approaches to doing the job.
3. To shed light on some of the key issues for effective general management in the NHS, with the emphasis on key relationships rather than on management processes such as planning.
4. To draw lessons that would help in the selection, development, evaluation and performance of general managers.

The research was published by the NHSTA as the Templeton Series on DGMs. The views expressed were those of the authors, and not necessarily of NHSTA. Nine Issue Studies were published in 1987 and mailed monthly to chairmen and DGMs.

1. DGMs and Chairmen: A Productive Relationship?
2. The DGM and Quality Improvement
3. DGMs and the DHA: Working with Members
4. Fully in the Picture? How DGMs Keep Informed
5. Managing with Doctors: Working Together?
6. DGMs and Region: Different Perspectives
7. DGMs and the Relationship between Districts and Units
8. Role and Progress of DGMs: An Overview
9. Learning to be a DGM (which included a

    Postscript: A Guide to the Selection of District General Managers and a Job Description for District General Managers to supplement the district's).

Methods

A sample of 20 DGMs were followed for two years from the early months of their appointment. The first five DGMs were chosen, to be as varied as possible in their jobs, from a management programme for DGMs at Templeton College. The aim then was to get the study started before the

186

full-time research associates could be appointed. The other 15 of the 20 were a stratified random sample designed to give the full sample maximum coverage of professional background and type of district. There was at least one member of the sample in every region in England and one in Wales. Four were from teaching districts.

The sample was stratified to ensure a much broader spread of career background than would have been obtained by a random sample. The sample consisted of: 7 administrators, 5 from outside the NHS including 3 from the armed services, 2 treasurers, 2 community physicians, 2 nurses and 2 hospital consultants.

The district populations were relatively evenly spread from just over 100 000 to well over 500 000. Revenue budgets ranged from under £20 million to over £100 million. The demographic characteristics of the districts were represented in almost the same proportions as in the OPCS clusters of 'demographic families' for the country as a whole.

Throughout the two years, the DGMs were asked about their views on their job, and about what they were doing. They were also asked to describe what they thought had gone well and what had gone badly, and why. Semi-structured questions were used, some of which were changed over time. There were special initial and final interviews and in between lengthy quarterly interviews. There were frequent, and often lengthy, telephone interviews at times to suit the DGM, which ranged from 8 a.m. to 9 p.m.. The average was 25 interviews with each DGM, with more frequent contact in the early months.

There were also interviews with chairmen and with some of the DGMs' principal contacts, the latter to ask questions about the subject of particular Issue Studies. A meeting of the DHA and of the district management board were observed in each district, and so were a few special meetings or seminars. Relevant documents were studied and previous agendas of the DMT compared with current agendas of the district management board.

The participating DGMs said that they had found the research process helpful because it stimulated them to take stock of what they were doing. It could also be helpful in difficult times to have a sympathetic listener.

Appendix B

1. Previous jobs? How long on present job?
2. What did you find most different about it?
3. What/who helped you to get where you are? Can you give examples?
4. What advice would you give someone aspiring to get a job like yours?
5. What do you see leadership as being?
6. Can you give some examples of leadership actions that you have seen?
7. Do you think of yourself as a leader?
8. How do you try to lead? influence? inspire others? (whichever of those words you feel comfortable with)
9. Can you give examples of where leadership is required in your job?
10. Do you think of yourself as a role model (example)? If so, does that influence how you act? If yes, can you illustrate?
11. Do you see any of your activities outside work as being leadership ones? If yes, do they also help you in leading at work? If yes, how?
12. (For women) Do you think women lead any differently? If yes, how?
13. What do you feel you have learned as a leader?
14. Still need to learn?

Notes and References

Introduction

1. Enoch Powell, for three years a Minister of Health, wrote in the early 1960s, that the NHS 'presents what must be the unique spectacle of an undertaking that is run down by everyone engaged in it'. That would be an extreme statement now, and no doubt was then, but unfortunately this distinctive characteristic of the NHS remains. Quotation from Joe Rogaly 'Hearts, Minds and Wallets', in the *Financial Times*, 22 January 1988, from Enoch Powell's book *Medicine and Politics*, (London: Pitman Medical, 1975).
2. One of the exceptions is Robert J. Maxwell and Victor Morrison (eds), 'Working with People' (King Edward's Hospital Fund for London, 1983).
3. This study was funded by the NHSTA, and published by them in 1987 and 1988 as the Templeton Series on DGMs in nine Issue Studies (see Appendix A).
4. Rosemary Stewart, Peter Smith, Jenny Blake and Pauline Wingate, 'The District Administrator in the National Health Service' (King Edward's Hospital Fund for London, 1980).
5. Papers published in James G. Hunt, Dian-Marie Hosking, Chester A. Schriesheim and Rosemary Stewart, *Leaders and Managers: International Perspectives on Managerial Behavior and Leadership* (New York: Pergamon Press, 1984).

1. Leadership

1. Unusually, an advertisement in the *Sunday Times*, 11 September 1988 for a UGM in Kingston and Esher Health Authority asked for 'demonstrable leadership quality'.
2. Rosemary Stewart, *The Reality of Management*, 2nd edn (London: Heinemann and Pan, 1985) and *The Reality of Organizations*, revised edn (Macmillan and Pan, 1985).
3. Warren Bennis and Burt Nanus, *Leaders: Five Strategies for Taking Charge* (New York: Harper & Row, 1985) pp. 89–90.
4. Bennis and Nanus, *Leaders*, pp. 92–3.
5. Gareth Morgan, *Riding the Waves of Change: Developing Managerial Competencies for a Turbulent World* (San Francisco: Jossey-Bass, 1988).
6. Warren Bennis, *The Unconscious Conspiracy: Why Leaders Can't Lead* (New York: AMACON, 1976) p. 15.
7. Douglas McGregor, *The Human Side of Enterprise* (New York: McGraw-Hill, 1960) p. 48. McGregor distinguished between Theory X, which he called the traditional view of motivation that people disliked work and therefore had to be coerced and controlled and Theory Y, which was that people will work willingly, in the right conditions.

189

8. J. de Kervasdoué, J. R. Kimberley and V. G. Rodwin, *The End of an Illusion: The Future of Health Policy in Western Industrialized Nations* (Berkeley: University of California, 1984).

9. West Midlands Regional Health Authority, 'Development of RHA "Core" Functions' (May 1987) p. 1.

10. The *Sunday Times*, 'Community Care at the Heart of a Winning Service' (September 1988) pp. H4–5.

11. Tom Peters, *Thriving on Chaos: Handbook for a Management Revolution*, (London: Macmillan, 1987) p. 416.

12. Peters, *Thriving on Chaos*, p. 414.

13. John Harvey-Jones, *Making it Happen: Reflections on Leadership* (London: Collins, 1988) pp. 112–13.

14. J. R. Meindl, S. B. Ehrlich and J. M. Dukerich, 'The Romance of Leadership', *Administrative Science Quarterly* (March 1985) pp. 78–102.

15. Tom Peters and Nancy Austin, *A Passion for Excellence: The Leadership Difference* (London: Collins, 1985).

Introduction to Part II

1. John P. Kotter, *The General Managers* (New York: Free Press, 1982).

2. John L. J. Machin and Charles H. S. Tai, 'Senior Managers Audit Their Own Communications', *Journal of Enterprise Management*, 2 (1979) pp. 75–85.

3. R. Beckhard, *Managing Change in Organizations: Participants' Workbook* (Cambridge, Mass.: Addison-Wesley, 1985); Roger Plant, *Managing Change and Making it Stick* (London: Fontana/Collins, 1987); T. Turrill, 'Change and Innovation: A Challenge for the NHS', *IHSM Management Series*, 10 (London: IHSM, 1986).

2. Leading Subordinates

1. Warren Bennis and Burt Nanus, *Leaders: Five Strategies for Taking Charge* (New York: Harper & Row, 1985) p. 80.

2. Readers who are unfamiliar with the word 'role' may wonder why it is sometimes used in place of 'job'. 'Role' means 'to play the part of', and is useful to convey that occupying a particular job can mean playing a particular role, as an actor does.

3. A good book about empowering one's subordinates is Peter Block, *The Empowered Manager: Positive Political Skills at Work* (San Francisco: Jossey-Bass, 1987).

4. John Harvey-Jones, *Making it Happen: Reflections on Leadership* (London: Collins, 1988) p. 65.

5. Templeton Series on District General Managers, directed by Rosemary Stewart, Issue Study No. 7, 'DGMs and the Relationship between District and Units' (NHSTA, 1987).

6. From the case study, 'The Outsider' by Sue Dopson, prepared for the NHSTA as part of the Templeton tracer study of DGMs.

7. Dopson, 'The Outsider'.
8. Harvey-Jones, *Making it Happen*, pp. 7–8.
9. Harvey-Jones, *Making it Happen*, pp. 67–8.

3. Leadership and Nurses

1. Tom Peters, *Thriving on Chaos: Handbook for a Management Revolution* (London: Macmillan, 1987).
2. D. Jones and C. Crossley-Holland, Matus I 'The Role of the Nursing Officer' (DHSS, 1981) showed that nursing officers did not regard the introduction or demonstration of new practices as applying to their jobs.
3. Rosemary Stewart, Peter Smith, Jenny Blake and Pauline Wingate, 'The District Administrator in the National Health Service' (King Edward's Hospital Fund for London, 1980).
4. Philip Strong and Jane Robinson, 'New Model Management: Griffiths and the NHS', Nursing Policy Studies Centre, University of Warwick (July 1988) p. 161.
5. R. Hutt, *et al.*, 'The Manpower Implications of Possible Changes in the Basic Nurse Training' (RCN Commission on Nurse Education, 1985).
6. R. Hutt, *et al.*, 'Attitudes, Jobs and Mobility of Qualified Nurses' (Brighton, Institute of Manpower Studies Report, 130, 1987).
7. P. Owens and H. Glennerster, 'The Nursing Management Functions after Griffiths: A second interim report 1986–7' (London School of Economics and Political Science and North West Thames Regional Health Authority, 1987) p. 28.
8. H. Koontz and C. O'Donnell, *Principles of Management: An Analysis of Management Functions*, 6th edn (New York: McGraw-Hill; Kogakusha: International Student edn, 1976) p. 346.
9. Owens and Glennerster, 'The Nursing Management Functions', pp. 24, 26.
10. Owens and Glennerster, 'The Nursing Management Functions', p. 42.
11. e.g. Goldstone, 'A Pointer to Quality – Monitor', *Nursing Times* (5 November, 1986) pp. 38–9; A. L. Kitson, 'Indicators of Quality in Nursing Care: an alternative approach', *Journal of Advanced Nursing*, II (1986) pp. 133–44; A. Pearson, 'The Burford Experience', *Nursing Mirror* (12 December, 1984); C. Wilson, *Hospital Medical Assurance* (Meditech, 1987); S. Wright, 'Patient-centred practice', *Nursing Times*, (1987) Vol. 83, No. 38, pp. 24–7.
12. P. J. Hibbs, 'Pressure Area Care for the City and Hackney Health Authority' (City and Hackney Health Authority, 1988) p. 3.
13. 'Patients are customers too', news item in *Marketing Business* (July 1988).
14. C. McLoughlin, 'Managing Change', paper for a RGM/DGM meeting, 3 December 1987.
15. R. W. Revans, *Action Learning in Hospitals: Diagnosis and Therapy* (London: McGraw-Hill, 1974). Part 1 of the book was published in 1964 as *Standards of Morale*.
16. J. A. Ball, L. A. Goldstone and M. M. Collier, 'Criteria for Care: The

Manual of the North West Staffing Levels Project' (Newcastle-upon-Tyne, Polytechnic Products, 1984); W. A. Telford, 'Determining Nurse Establishment', *Health Services Manpower Review*, 5 (November 1979).

4. Leadership and Doctors

1. This section, in particular, draws upon the relevant issue study from the Templeton Series on DGMs, directed by Rosemary Stewart, Issue Study No. 5, 'Managing with Doctors: Working Together?' (NHSTA, 1987).
2. NHSTA, 'Doctors and Management Development: Policy Proposals from the National Health Service Training Authority' (NHSTA, 1988) p. 7.
3. W. J. McQuillan, 'Doctors as Managers: a Personal View', in Freda Eskin, *Personal Perspectives on Being an NHS Manager* (University of Manchester, Centre for Professional Development, 1988).
4. John Lewis, 'Clinical Directorates Soon for All Acute NHS Hospitals?', *The Lancet*, (May 1988) p. 1060.
5. NHSTA, 'Doctors and Management Development', p. 2.
6. Quoted by Nicholas Timmins in 'To heal, and then to count the cost', *Independent*, (16 December, 1987).
7. John Harvey-Jones, *Making it Happen: Reflections on Leadership* (London: Collins, 1988) p. 126.

5. Sharing the Leadership

1. Templeton Series on DGMs, directed by Rosemary Stewart, Issue Study No. 1, 'DGMs and Chairmen: A Productive Relationship?' (NHSTA, 1986).
2. R. M. Belbin, *Management Teams: why they succeed or fail* (London: Heinemann, 1981).

6. Leadership and the DHA

1. Templeton Series on DGMs, directed by Rosemary Stewart, Issue Study No. 3, 'DGMs and the DHA: Working with Members' (NHSTA, 1986) p. 7.
2. Secretaries of State for Health, Wales, Northern Ireland and Scotland, *Working for Patients* (Her Majesty's Stationery Office, January 1989).
3. Quoted in NAHA, 'Acting with Authority (NAHA, 1986) p. 3.
4. *Working with Patients* pp. 64–5.
5. Charlotte Williamson, 'Authority Members and Standards of Non-Clinical Care', *Hospital and Health Services Review* (January 1986) p. 19.
6. Templeton Series on DGMs, directed by Rosemary Stewart, Issue Study No. 3, p. 9.
7. Cf. Cedric Sandford, 'Bath Gives Lead to its Members', *The Health Service Journal* (5 March 1987); The University of Birmingham Health Services Management Centre, 'The Role of the Health Authority and

its Members: Post Griffiths, Newcastle Health Authority' (Health Services Management Centre, University of Birmingham, 1986).
8. NAHA, 'Acting with Authority'.
9. Sandford, 'Bath Gives Lead', p. 278.
10. Warren Kinston, 'The District Health Authority,' working paper (Brunel Institute of Organization and Social Studies, 1986).
11. Anne Spencer, *On the Edge of the Organization: The Role of the Outside Director* (Chichester, John Wiley, 1983) p. 67.

7. Leadership in the Region–District Relationship

1. This and other RGM quotation is taken from the RGM interviews held in the summer of 1987 for the Templeton study of DGMs. See also Templeton Series on DGMs, directed by Rosemary Stewart, Issue Study No. 6 'DGMs and Region: Different Perspectives' (NHSTA, 1987).

8. External Leadership

1. John Harvey-Jones, *Making it Happen: Reflections on Leadership* (London: Collins, 1988) p. 224.
2. A. F. Long and S. Harrison (eds), *Health Services Performance: Effectiveness and Efficiency* (London: Croom Helm, 1985) p. 97.
3. Long and Harrison (eds), *Health Services Performance*, p. 102. Jack Hallas, 'CHCs in Action: a Review' (London: Nuffield Provincial Hospitals Trust, 1976).
4. Gordon Chase and Elizabeth C. Reveal, *How to Manage in the Public Sector* (Reading, Mass.: Addison-Wesley, 1983) p. 129.
5. Organisation for Economic Co-operation and Development, 'Administration as Service – The Public as Client' (Paris: OECD, 1987).
6. R. Rhodes, 'Developing the Public Service Orientation', *Local Government Studies* 63–73 (May–June 1987) p. 68.
7. David King, 'Health', in Drew Clode, Christopher Parker and Stuart Ethrington, *Towards the Sensitive Bureaucracy: Consumers' Welfare and the New Pluralism* (Aldershot: Gower, 1987) p. 57.
8. Chase and Reveal, *How to Manage*, pp. 128–30.
9. Long and Harrison (eds), *Health Services Performance*, p. 102.
10. The *Sunday Times*, 'Community Care at the Heart of a Winning Service' (11 August 1988).
11. King, 'Health'.
12. Karin Eriksen, *Human Services Today*, 2nd edn (Reston, Virginia: Reston Publishing, 1981).
13. Christine Hogg, 'The Public and the NHS' (Association of Community Health Councils for England and Wales, 1986) p. 46.

9. Fifteen Young Leaders

1. Bernard M. Bass, *Stogdill's Handbook of Leadership: A Survey of Theory and Research*, revised and expanded edn (New York: Free Press, 1981) p. 499.

11. Managing the Job and Yourself

1. Warren Bennis and Burt Nanus, *Leaders: Five Strategies for Taking Charge* (New York: Harper & Row, 1985) p. 56.
2. *Making it Happen: Reflections on Leadership* (London: Collins, 1988) p. 20.
3. Rosemary Stewart, *Choices for the Manager: A Guide to Managerial Work and Behaviour* (Maidenhead: McGraw-Hill, 1982).
4. There are a number of useful books on the management of time, for example: John Adair, *How to Manage Your Time* (Guildford: Talbot Adair, 1987); Sally Garratt, *Manage Your Time* (London: Fontana/Collins, 1985); Alan Lakein, *How to Get Control of Your Time and Your Life* (Aldershot: Gower, 1984). These are useful 'how to do it' books; a different kind of book is Rosemary Stewart, *Managers and Their Jobs: A Study of the Similarities and Differences in the Ways Managers Spend Their Time*, 2nd edn (London: Macmillan, 1988) which reports a study of how 160 managers spent their time, illustrates different forms of diary-keeping and the lessons that the participant managers drew about using their time more effectively.
5. This was the title of Issue Study 4 in the Templeton Series of DGMs, directed by Rosemary Stewart, so readers are referred to that for a fuller discussion.
6. Sune Carlson, *Executive Behaviour: A Study of the Workload and Working Methods of Managing Directors* (Stockholm: Strömbergs, 1951).
7. Suresh Srivastva and Frank J. Barrett, 'Foundations for Executive Integrity: Dialogue, Diversity, Development', in Suresh Srivastva and Associates, *Executive Integrity: The Search for High Human Values in Organizational Life* (San Francisco: Jossey-Bass, 1988) pp. 298–9.

12. Managing Yourself

1. Michael Maccoby, *The Leader: A New Face for American Management* (New York: Simon & Schuster, 1981) p. 54.
2. This, and some of the following quotations are taken from Issue Study No. 9 'Learning to be a DGM', Templeton Series on DGMs, directed by Rosemary Stewart (NHSTA, 1987).
3. A useful collection of papers on self-development, given at a conference sponsored by the MSC in 1986, is Mike Pedler, John Burgoyne and Tom Boydell, *Applying Self-development in Organizations* (New York: Prentice Hall, 1988).
4. Katherine C. Briggs, and Isabel Briggs Myers, *Myers–Briggs Type Indicator* (Palo Alto, California: Consulting Psychologists Press, 1976).
5. Mike Pedler, John Burgoyne and Tom Boydell, *A Manager's Guide to Self-Development*, 2nd edn (Maidenhead: McGraw-Hill, 1978).
6. D. A. Kolb, K. M. Rubin, and J. M. McIntyre, *Organizational Psychology: An Experiential Approach* (Englewood Cliffs, N.J.: Prentice-Hall, 1971).

Index